MORE PRAISE FOR

SORROWLAND ORACLE

"Ayodele Nzinga is a force of nature. The poems of SorrowLand Oracle are philosophical sermons of fire, works designed to breathe in life and shut down evil. These are hot prayers, bold and demonstrative, to be broadcast over the spilled blood of history. Be careful with these poems. By reading them, something may get conjured."

JAMES CAGNEY
author of *Black Steel Magnolias in the Hour of Chaos Theory*, 2019 winner of the PEN Oakland Josephine Miles Award

"Water-laden and resolute these poems speak to the depth and reach of the Black Lives Matter movement; they chronicle the history of Black people who have been subjected to tremendous degradation but have still maintained their humanity and love which is the force that drives them to keep fighting against injustice. Ayodele's poems make you feel lashes but they also restore and guide you forward to dance with the drums."

OPAL PALMER ADISA
author of 20 books of poems, stories, novels, and children's books

"Ayodele's words stirs souls. The poems she's given us here dig into the grit and gristle of life while casting a quality of light that allows readers to see and understand their, our humanity. With this book, she shows and proves why we call her Wordslanger."

LISA D. GRAY
Our Voices Our Stories SF

"*SorrowLand Oracle* is for those who have eyes to see. "game" is my favorite as it reminds me of Dr. Nzinga, it reminds me of me, it reminds me of the brilliance of our ancestors and their dominating spirit to survive in spite of it all. "game" is resilience. "game" is Black people, game is Black culture, and "game" is the essence of Nzinga's spiritual, political, cultural writing that can't stop, won't stop! "game" is Ayodele Nzinga's determination. It is beauty!"

NEFERTITTI JACKMON
Cultural Strategist

"Nzinga wields words like a sharp knife ... a quick turn peels away surfaces, allowing air and light into deep wounds. Personal and yet grand in scope, they sing when read aloud and longer in the mind, revealing more upon each reading."

CHARLIE LEVIN
The One Truthiness

"Some poetic letters are an ancestral and strategic life blueprint, a history lesson from middle earth, a Black gaze signaling a call to arms, or gently bequeathed ocean wisdom. Dr. Ayodele Nzinga's new poetic offering *SorrowLand Oracle* encompasses all of these notions ... and more. At its core it is a prayer anthem. For the ages. Along its letters the reader will traverse through emotional trails of comfort and rage, the challenge of self awareness and responsibility, and the sorrow of a soul being excavated and placed upon a bright sacred table. *SorrowLand Oracle* is a search mission, and a revealing, of Black truth and life. It is the prophetic reckoning that must always precede a recompense of justice. Perhaps Dr. Nzinga says it best when she writes, "We must remember. We must be the river." I am certain that *SorrowLand Oracle* is something akin to a divine sea scroll. Penned by the fiery Black fingers of Dr. Nzinga at the behest of an ocean deep ancient Black soul, a caretaker of all given understanding and truths."

REGINA EVANS
abolitionist, winner of the Jefferson Award

NOMADIC PRESS

OAKLAND

111 FAIRMONT AVENUE
OAKLAND, CA 94611

BROOKLYN

475 KENT AVENUE #302
BROOKLYN, NY 11249

WWW.NOMADICPRESS.ORG

MASTHEAD

FOUNDING PUBLISHER
J. K. FOWLER

ASSOCIATE EDITOR
MICHAELA MULLIN

DESIGN
JEVOHN TYLER NEWSOME

MISSION STATEMENT

Through publications, events, and active community participation, Nomadic Press collectively weaves together platforms for intentionally marginalized voices to take their rightful place within the world of the written and spoken word. Through our limited means, we are simply attempting to help right the centuries' old violence and silencing that should never have occurred in the first place and build alliances and community partnerships with others who share a collective vision for a future far better than today.

INVITATIONS

Nomadic Press wholeheartedly accepts invitations to read your work during our open reading period every year. To learn more or to extend an invitation, please visit: www.nomadicpress.org/invitations

DISTRIBUTION

Orders by teachers, libraries, trade bookstores, or wholesalers:

Nomadic Press Distribution
orders@nomadicpress.org
(510) 500-5162

Small Press Distribution
spd@spdbooks.org
(510) 524-1668 / (800) 869-7553

SorrowLand Oracle
First edition © 2020 by Ayodele Nzinga
Second edition © 2022 by Ayodele Nzinga

This book was made possible by a loving community of chosen family and friends, old and new.

For author questions or to book a reading at your bookstore, university/school, or alternative establishment, please send an email to info@nomadicpress.org.

Cover art: Nedra T. Williams, Olokun Priestess (Conjure Collage Art & Design)

Published by Nomadic Press, 111 Fairmount Avenue, Oakland, California 94611

First printing, 2020

Second printing, 2022

Library of Congress Cataloging-in-Publication Data

Title: **SorrowLand Oracle**
p. cm.
Summary: *SorrrowLand Oracle* by Ayodele Nzinga is a compendium of spells, incantations, prayers, and their translations into the event of being Black in modernity while standing at the crossroads of revolutionary transformation and the birthing of a new paradigm on the eve of an apocalypse.

[1. POETRY / American / African American & Black. 2. POETRY / Women Authors. 3. HISTORY / African American & Black 4. POETRY / Subjects & Themes / Inspirational & Religious. 5. POETRY / American / General.] I. III. Title.

LIBRARY OF CONGRESS CONTROL NUMBER: 2021948411

ISBN: 9781955239134

SORROWLAND ORACLE

AYODELE NZINGA

SORROWLAND ORACLE

AYODELE NZINGA

**NOMADIC
PRESS**

contents

foreword
  by Cat Brooks
preface
introduction

right handed poems

ink

that new millennium dime

reading guide

foreword

The first time I met ayodele "wordslanger" nzinga was auditioning for her. New to Oakland and nervous, I climbed the steps to her house... no one warned me and no one could have prepared me for what was on the other side of that door. Locs flowing, cigarette burning, and ancestors working, she sat down on the couch across from me and said, "Go." And go I did. When ayodele commands you to move, you move.

That was 13 years ago. Over the last decade, plus I have been the grateful beneficiary of the genius of ayodele nzinga... even in the moments I would have preferred to remain blissfully ignorant. But ignorant artists are nothing ayo suffers. And if you are lucky enough for her to actually consider you an artist, your fee—and your mandate—is overstanding the power of your craft.

Black words on a white page. At first glance, they appear to be just that. Words on a page. But when those words come from a warrior, a griot, a prophet, a muse... when those words come from a woman named "slanger"—they are weapons of war. Tools of liberation. The soundtrack to Black bodies marching through streets, choking down tear gas, demanding recognition of our humanity. They are our prayers, our meditations, and our mournings.

For years, repeatedly, ad nauseam, ayo has said to me, "I. do. not. march." She. doesn't. have. to. She slangs lyrics that motivate the marchers and mystify the oppressors. Her battlefield is at the computer, on the page, and behind the microphone.

Despite, far too often, being an afterthought of modern-day organizers, the fact is there are no movements without artists. Artists pull back the veil and force us to look when we would rather avert our eyes. Artists introduce revolution to the Thankstaking dinner table when the family would rather discuss the weather. Artists are the mirrors to our collective consciousness and they are not afraid to shatter it to make the point.

The point of ayodele's pen shatters things: thoughts, ideas, comfort zones, generational curses. Then, with the grace and patience of a sage, she invites you to collectively rebuild it all over again … but better.

The shattering of all you thought you knew? A type of death for most artists, for most people past a certain age … present company included. But!!!! The resurrection is a promise of doing what you do best … better.

If you have ever been in her physical presence, you know that ayodele can strip your soul naked with a look. Her words are no less fierce. But they are also a gift. A clarion call. A North Star. An unflinching and unapologetic accounting of the stories of Black folk, our collective intergenerational trauma, and the glory of our resilience and resistance. They are a road map to liberation. And perhaps, most importantly, they are a huge "fuck you" to the white supremacist patriarchy … and anyone who rocks with it.

As someone who does regularly march in these streets, her words are the armor I wear to keep me safe, the soundtrack to our footsteps, and the pendulum of accountability I swing in an effort to clock if the ancestors are pleased with our efforts.

"Pray with your hands moving," she often quips at me. That is what her work is. A moving prayer for our people. An exorcism of our trauma and a reinstatement of our glory.

ayodele "wordslanger" nzinga is our 21st century griot. May you find inspiration, healing, accountability, and the mandate of the ancestors in these pages.

She Arts...

With revolutionary imagination and love,

CAT BROOKS

preface
to the new edition

Communique from the blue ball
star date: pandemic: year 2

these are my questions:

what's the penalty for watching drunk children piss in the ocean?
what's a tree worth—if it's the only one left?

bayo akomolafe tells us, "times are urgent—let us slow down"

in the narrative of ifa, these are the times of babalu aye.

babalu aye/obaluwaye is the orisha of pandemic, healing, and cleansing.

when babalu aye is active in the world, it signals a time of change
predicated by imbalance.

we are to stay inside our ile/our home/our temple. we must go inside
and cleanse while babalu aye is walking in the streets of the world,
cleansing and pruning. he is said not to favor insolence, the immoral,
arrogant, or wicked. change is a process of death and rebirth.

change begins within. old habits of mind must pass away for change to occur.

the door is open.

what lies between us and a new paradigm?

the liminal, the unfixed, the void of the unknown.

we can neither dismantle the master's house nor build a more fitting one with the available tools. even the goal is questionable.

the goal is not a new version of the status quo or a quest to center marginalized folk in this reality.

we seek new materials. we require new tools to build new things of which we have not yet conceived. to conceive what comes next, we must be willing to quit remaking the things that stop thriving.

the door is open.

can we traverse the void?

as the west coast burns, historic weather events hit the east coast and midwest. as the south is inundated with storms of biblical proportion, hate crimes rise, refugees hug borders in search of relief, and wealth gaps widen as crime stats soar. hospitals swell with covid patients; thoughts of rationed care are entertained; as we navigate multiple shortages, we are restless and perturbed that someone, anyone, won't wave a magic wand and fix it—now. even if that means just put it back the way it was—a zero-sum status quo where every problem that seems so urgent in this moment existed before babalu aye made his presence known amongst us.

we are uncomfortable with unknowing—we find comfort in what we think we know. we are so full of knowing we have little space for questions about how we know, who/what taught us what we think we know and why. such thoughts invite existential dread.

we know change as a constant, yet we fear it like death.

we want change. we are afraid of changing.

charlie levin says we won't change because we need to be sure of where grandma has breakfast.

i think—the question is moot if grandma and i don't make it to morning.

my granny would have called charlie's thinking: holding on to the devil you know.

when former slave, solly two kings, burns down the mill in august wilson's play, gem of the ocean, caesar wilks, the antihero, asks where the people will work now.

solly says he doesn't know, but they won't be working at the racist mill.

that's change.

as i travel in alignment with babalu aye, guarding my footsteps and the steps of those that cross mine, i have written rituals to inform mill burning.

matches not included.

ayodele "wordslanger" **nzinga**

introduction

this moment is not our home nor can it be our testament

I have only the vaguest recall of learning to read & write, only vibrant memories of doing both from a young age. language & memory intersect in me. my life is measured by being transformed by things i've read, things i've written, the memory of those moments, & the doors they opened in me, bringing, tugging, pulling, leading me to the river(s) that lead to the ocean(s). my work, life, & world(s) are connected firmly to the ocean, ebbs & flows, powerful movement, its unfathomable depth with abundant life beneath the surface.

words saved my life. poetry, narratives, myths, tall tales, & history were my friends from the beginning; safer than a world where things that should not happen did. i retreated into the world of words to survive the world. in my retreat, like maya angelou, i devoured the world in silence. the words of historians, poets, playwrights, scholars from antiquity through negritude, the harlem renaissance, the black arts movement, & the texts of the political movements that provide the context for literary epochs shaped me into a race woman.

reading from all the canons suggested there was more than the western view of the world, & the thought opened a space in me that is receptive to stray majick. i read origin stories from around the globe, myths of the "may have been," history on other continents before america, & the probability of a columbus. paulo freire offered the world as a text that can be read. that has always intrigued me as all texts invite critique. if the world can be read—we can rewrite it. professor rachel martin, who offers thoughtful analyses of freire, told me, "language creates the world & then hides its role in having done so." the power of words to create reality is undeniable. the truth created in words is incarnate. for me, words are synonymous with august wilson's description of fire—they can kill or heal.

memory and language are spells

"sticks & stones will break your bones, but words will never hurt you" is a verbal amulet, the spell used to conjure protection from hexes cast using words. "let there be light" is the origin story of light cutting dark on command, the commencement of the eternal & ongoing struggle between the two. words are agreements, building blocks for understanding, inspiration, terror-inducing, balm, weapons, our prayers to existence enabling all our whys, & all the possible answers.

first, there was the word. no action begins without a thought. no thought can be shared or amplified into action in the absence of words or some alternate currency, enabling the exchange of thought. communication proceeds our contemplation & sparks our eventual action. i posit the world is made from & maintained by words, both said & unsaid.

my medium is words, found & saved ripe phrases, remnants of broken understandings, neologisms, reclaimed words, weaponized words made holy, seeking overstanding, sent out into the world naked to collect more knowing. i intend to use all the tools gifted me to be in conversation with the world(s) i inhabit. i understand the multiverse as a living organism we co-create. we are all the creators of the reality we inhabit. our words & thoughts have power. in the words of my grandmother, nettie m brown, "nothing beats misunderstanding like being understood."

george bernard shaw says, "the single biggest problem in communication is the illusion that it has taken place." charlie levin offers this bon mot, "between what i think, what i want to say, what i think i say, what i say, what you want to hear, what you hear, what you think you understand, what you want to understand, & what you finally understand—there are nine possibilities of not understanding each other."

i write to communicate my understanding of a world with few absolutes, dazzling beauty, barbaric cruelty, fractured by fictions, yearning for meaning, substance—gasping for joy. i invite you to the world of my boneyard soldiers dying to live, where grandma's hands & collard greens are holy items. i open for you the world where the wind is a constant, in need of harnessing, so it can be coached into blowing for us. in these pages, i welcome you to the ocean, the land of teaspoons against bulldozers, & tales of unlikely magicians resolutely walking a winding road to a new world. walk with us, wear our dreams, feel their weight. black dreamers & other magicians come to witness us dressed as ourselves & sprinkle these pages with your innerstandings. i write to conjure the dismantling of the webs woven to hobble humanity, for the dead who whisper to me, & children not yet born.

if tomorrow still needs freedom songs—i want to be one.

lately, clear messages from the universe say we are at a portal. at this moment, many things that seem impossible are very likely. the shape of the majick in the offing requires our hands. the veil is lifted. the year 2020 ruptured existence. can we wedge an opening wide enough to birth a new paradigm? the spells needed will require us to raise the new from the chaos surrounding our ways of being & witnessing the death of familiar but extinct forms. we must adopt a posture of change & give it a language we overstand. my offering to our ritual unfolding is my words.

some authors want readers. i want an army. language needs an army to exist—you can't have an army if you can't feed them. an army has to eat. *SorrowLand Oracle* is food for my army. i serve mental groceries. may these words be bread & bullets that you hold somewhere between sermon & prayer.

in the house of Olokun
there are no empty plates
cups overflow

praying with my hands moving—

ayodele "wordslanger" **nzinga**

right handed poems

lifted

some will not come

they won't hear the drum

the cannon roars

the air is thin

the time is always now

marching believers know this

they are lacing their boots

uphill forward

there is no other way

never has been in the land of cotton

ten thousand feet eleven million dreams marching

uphill forward out of the ocean

trying to swim on dry land in diminishing potential

some will not hear the drum

but the battlefield is clear

there are no batons to pass

all hands are called for

the bell tolls

stones have been thrown

the time is always now

in the land of
skinny godz

in the land of skinny godz

there is naked famine &

bottomless want

the people wander

eyes closed

voiceless

afraid of punishment

toes to the line

ignoring the crimes

standing in lines

praying

better times

skinny godz don't

hear

they don't answer

blood dripping from eyes

hands in

their pants

at the crossroads

of meaning & power

they don't want you to

see them unrobed

lying & stealing

legs spread

syphilitic infected with

polytics

trying to assassinate

a paradigm shift

rewarding those who follow

targeting those who drift

to the left

or live & die

to do right

proclaiming

drink dirt

call it water

fouling the natural order

skinny godz

made of plastic &

napalm dangling

from chains of depleted uranium

burning the necks of the desperate

while guilt nests in their craniums

like ruthless roof wrens

skinny godz

with no faith in their fate

no trust in the work of their hands

overstanding their lack of innocence

sure they have sinned

in deed & by omission

in the land of skinny godz

no revelation without permission

& or prescription

the money is in the nurturing

of your condition

no cures no miracles

just tithes & gifts

no miracles no cures

better comes after this

more tithes

more gifts

live on your knees

eyes towards heaven

remember only the

gifts & tithes

to a broke ass

skinny god who

has an accountant

counting on what

you can bring him

to manifest manna

for a constant hunger

while the people wander

in famine suffering want

bathing in the dirt

dreaming of water

eyes closed

voiceless

afraid of punishment

towing the line

ignoring the crimes

prostrate

praying for better times

skinny godz

don't hear they

don't answer

bag life

the bags in carts on bikes over weary shoulders

bags that mark them as without

outside unhoused wanderers carrying

their lives in bags

/?/do they carry their important papers

do they carry the warmer sweater

when the sun beats down

remembering the promise of winter

is always kept

do they carry

the last scraps of

membership in society capitalist

or maybe their sunday best in hopes

of needing to be dressed up

ready to become one of

those inside whose lives

are not confined to bags

rather they are free to

consume more than they need

stepping over the unwashed

on their way to inside

/?/ do the homeless

carry their last christmas

warm with family

enabling backwards glances at

together once upon a nowgone time

/?/ do they carry the what if(s)

& why me(s) or were they left

behind with changes of shoes

clean underwear predictable tomorrows & warm beds

/?/ do they carry muted memories of a life

without so much baggage

what do homeless people carry in the bags

/?/do they carry mementos of unruly lives

their dreams of tomorrow shattered

& broken down

so they fit

inside black plastic

stack

neatly in dirty bins stacked

beside tents under

freeway overpasses as passers-by

pass on their way

to their cozy

inside spaces

far away

from

bag life

#youwillnotkillmetoday

death will come

on the day it wants

dressed as it pleases

at the time it chooses

death will come

of that

there is little doubt

how it will be received

is the matter here

#youwillnotkillmetoday

with ignorance

or hate

steeped brewed & held close

you will not kill me

because melanin keeps

writing things you thought

you had erased

you will not kill my longing to be free

or my demands for equity

#youwillnotkillmetoday

there are traps by my

front door

armed guards at the

back of my mind

lest you try to

slip in with me

unaware today

is not your day

if old age comes

soft to drape me

in forever i will

graciously away

but today is not that day

miles to travel

more forward to draw

from the mud

more errands for my ancestors

more clever cartography

more dancing tomorrow

from fractured todays

& hard lived yesterdays

i have grown tough skin

over my hope

i water it with pragmatism

i am vigilant & will

not be set upon unaware

i anticipate you in my dreams

i have drawn a circle in

salt around your intentions

& wrapped a prayer in white

cloth delivered it to a tree

that knows your name

i have talked to the dust

& the wind about you

& they whisper my name

before yours as life naturally

precedes death

#youwillnotkillmetoday

i am the promise risen
from the ocean
i am what grows outside
the fences you build
i am the rising whine at
the back of your worried
fretful mind (yes
the other shoe will drop)
bells are for tolling
as each dog has a sunrise
suns set on all houses
this is not your day
today
 i walk upright unafraid
cakewalking on oppression
drumming for justice
walking against the wind

up every hill since the good ship jesus & plymouth rock

i am the sword & the stone

carrying darkness like a banner

inviting storm

i am chaos & creation

i am

my machetes are sharp

my powder is dry

i have left yucca for

the left-handed child

iron in my

right pocket honey

in my hand

#youwillnotkillmetoday

i have banished you from

the land of my dreams

i want not i suffer not

i am the living circle

unbroken

i am

left-handed child

i dreamed of the left-handed

child standing in the middle of

the road

i have been dreaming about

preaching on milk cartons

most of my dreams

come from the ocean

my sleep is a classroom

my teachers

are mostly dead

they speak

because i listen

i dreamed of the left-handed

child standing in the middle

of the road

i have dreamed of

a line stretching

back to the beginning

how can a line be

a maze

snatch a people out of a

paradigm set them

outside of existence

& majick must

occur if they

are to go on

they must be protagonist

crossing a desert

forced into the labyrinth

within another

man's logic

a straight line

up out across

an ocean

i have dreamed

me looking up

from olokun's

waiting room with the

ibos singing on the bottom

woke to find myself

overstanding

seeing from above

seals broken

things revealed

i dreamed of the left-handed

child standing in the middle

of the road

***

eya texted me

confirmation

a push in the small

of the back

***

up the hill

staying to the right

of the left-handed

child leaving yucca

anise brandy &

canary seed

at his feet

***

omi tutu

ile tutu

ona tutu

tutu eshu

tutu orisha

***

staying to the

right side of the road

bowing to the left

handed child

armed with bow & arrow

opening

the door for me

in conversation with god

do you talk to god

do you listen when
god answers do you
overstand god's will
god demands
you see god's work
you hear
god's voice vibrating
penetrating
the surface of the
ocean echoing
phantoms below
feel god's power
blowing the wind
leveling the plains
moving mountains
opening skies

hanging the moon

pulling back the sun

do you listen to god

changing the seasons

stringing the stars

holding up the firmament

dressing the trees

birthing

in the midst of

burying

mightily eternally

watching weighing measuring

do you listen to the holder

of scales the owner of darkness

the provider of light the

alpha the omega

the beginning

circling the end

do you listen

discomfort

*"your belief & my reality
may be mutually exclusive"*

i tried

to paint the picture

they shuddered

i needed

them to see

they averted their eyes

i needed

them to hear

they put their hands over their ears

they say

they want to understand

but they can't stay in the room

too much history

too much pain

too much fear

too much

for them to hold the thought of me

broken

but moving

left for dead

but breathing

dismissed

but still present

they can't

inspect the wounds

no prescription for my trauma

no room

in their days

filled with ease to catalogue

how my life bleeds

they want

clean hands

but blood is everywhere

they want

to sleep at night

i have no resting place

must hit the marks

that move as i approach

they say

they set a place

i can't find the table

i am here

at the margin

looking for

the opening in the conversation

that is large enough for all of me

i try to paint the picture

but some

need their ease

more that justice

need peace of mind

i have never had

need to remain secure safe

to be sane

i have never

been secure or safe

they claim the right

to be safe

code for the

absence of me

& my discomfort

the closing of jesus

i saw jesus break dancing on
a corner in west oakland
right before the banks came
to steal black folk's homes
must have been a warning
he was beautiful homeless funky
dust flying from his dreads as he
contorted his self into shapes
that defied reason with syncopation
that was undeniable beating out
the truth in a dance of the times
jesus
ditty bop bopping hyphy breaking
crunkly popping locks moon walking
juking his joints sliding electrically
to the holy ghost
dancing on the
corner of pine & 11th
facing the old train station

(it ain't there no more—condos)

or the freeway that roars like

an ocean at night early

morning making music

with beeping trucks

of waste at the space

where the old center

of the world collided with

the end of the world

recycling the used to make way

for the shiny & new between

lines of hungry children

marching single file to

free breakfast lunch programs

or maybe he was on the corner

newton died on dancing

while parents search for

work that can't be found

pack up houses after being

baptized with balloons full of

piss water tossed

by colonial goons

to be reborn drowning

underwater landless with jesus

c-walking on the corner of 14th

& willow under the mural

before laying down in the middle

of the street on the yellow

line it must

have been a sign but

didn't nobody pay attention

but i saw it

in the middle of the day

heat rising off the asphalt

jesus barefoot dancing

near the recycling center

(closed now—shut down

because it fed the unwashed

pushing carts full of waste

from the shiny & new)

jesus

best not dance there

no more wonder what

happened to dancing jesus

must have been a message

but didn't nobody hear it

as the trucks left with the

people & the dreams leaving

me to wonder where jesus

is dancing now

a young man
stood

a young man stood

he said he spoke as

a child—speaking in

a room filled w/women

who had lost children

a child stood to speak

as a son in a room filled

w/mothers who had lost sons

he spoke as a grandson

in a room where mamie till's

testimony still stained

the air he spoke of life

in a room w/ oscar grant's

mother & grandmother

speaking the story of

how women fill

rooms looking after children

husbands & fathers who

have gone missing women walking

wounded by a system that's

eaten their men buried

them living in decaying schools

commercial prisons

acres upon acres of

graves both deep &

shallow final resting

atop potential stilled

in a room full of women

a grandson stood

to represent

the missing men

stood in

support of crying

women as we wept

many praises on his

head sweet breath

moving chest

bless his beating heart

standing

warm living

our hopeful

dreams dreamed

as we

weep

over their death

bobby hutton park

the defermerys are alive

says the beige councilwoman

they may be living but

bobby hutton is dead

we have renamed the park

to keep him alive

surely, you understand

life & death

eternally binary

we are binary people

alive or dead

black or white

in or out of favor

out of office

out of the city

on the other side

out of time

out of life

outside of life

bobby hutton is dead

denzil dowell is dead

i hope they claimed a token

for denzil somewhere in

richmond i have cried

offered prayer & ritual

hallowing sanctifying center st

after the sage burned out

& the egungun danced

we claimed the corner

baptized it in the name

of godz who favor drumz

we let huey know

we remember

to remember

we lay claim to him

in all his parts

elevating the genius accepting

that flawed humans are the

handz of the godz

we remember to remember

a bowl of honey by the

cactus in the yard

we pray for the flower

we pray for the thorns

& warriors who sacrificed

like graceful ocean divers

suiciding burning like fire

knowing they were never

meant to be slaves

their death marks the places

we crossed over

overcame

transcended

ascended

spirits walking waiting

to be claimed

we have renamed

defermery & given it to

bobby hutton so that his spirit

has a place to grow

the beige
lady says

you can have the trees

they are already ours
we have claimed them
she cannot give us what we
have taken
we don't want wampum
popcorn & beads we have taken
what we need—
a place to remember
quicksilver crossings
ember becoming
spark turned flame
the passion of
slaves who refuse
burning like fire

burn baby burn

we praise the spark

we honor the flame

long live bobby hutton

room full of
broken birds

the new born still talk to the dead

the dead go as the new are born

entering exiting

a room full of broken birds

called life

we are born dying

the young man said it

life brimming in

his eyes

his beard full

untouched by gray

his life still full

of possible un dulled by

broken birds flapping ineptly

some refuse to fly

others are all beak

some without feathers

horror stories

amongst the beautifully plumed

the aerially erudite

who paint themselves upon sky

like sunlight

high above the

smell of

birdshit

yet bound by the same rules

all will perish

none are forever

the aviary is all there is

there is no more

& sorry

nothing less

than feathers

blood

squawks from fledglings

trying to influence pecking orders

that melt & mean less

than nothing as dead

go & new are born

in this room full of broken birds

we live

in the shadow of

our own limitations

our isms

doubts

mean fears

desperate dreams

all flapping wildly in

a room full of broken birds

where ideology

is born & dies

to be reinvented on the

beaks of

new birds

flying high

on old ideas

they just hatched

in a room full of broken birds

afterthought

first you hear that boom

                          in the distance

your eyes find the sky

                marvel at the rain of iridescence

                you quiver inside

                realize godz alive

but you won't live forever

you start to weigh

the sins the lies the places

you were willing to bend

to blend in to slip in under

the wire your mind wanders

as you contemplate the fire

wondering if the good you

could have done would have

been enough & like a moving

hand your life written on shimmering

sand finds it's a winding sheet

there's a band & whispering

behind the fans

                                 you can't hear the band

you exit wondering

what it is they're whispering

old men

blue black creased

by living

gin on their breath

underneath the

the crushing weight

of being born invisible

5 dollar cigars &

knowing in their mouths

long eyes pained

by memory

grown in the shadow of years

stacked atop one another

toppling down now

to spell out their

existences leanly

marking thin

lives running like

a river over the shore

so much

so much

not enough light

waiting on the taste of justice

overdue

turned sages holding

knowledge like rosary beads

prayed over with

bloody hands

bony knuckled

holding up the moon

to witness

smoke curling

off ashes of

burning dreams

game

one in a million

or one working harder

than one million

always on looking

for a crack in the door

lucid dreamer

taking notes

one more mountain

knowing

there is another beyond

hungry

tapped into the infinite

growing

vision exceeds grasp

distilling lessons

defining falling

as an opportunity

diamond grind

radiance reflecting

inner shine

dedicated

sometimes tired never weary

eyes on the prize

got grit

determined

fluid knowing what

won't bend probably

break

the real thing

hard in the paint

above the rim

unlikely candidate

certain to win

refuses to fail

playing the game

immaculately

nothing but

stars above

this hustle

ink

canon

in the bosom

smelling like milk

knowing this is as close

to the honey

as they gonna let you get

it's bitter to the taste

inside

the house

walking on the bones

somebody write this story

tell what it cost

brown eyed dreamers

crossing continents

with spoons

instead of knives

hungry

everything that was

gone

nothing means

what it meant

nobility turned savagery

by ethnographers' pen strokes

un tongued & stripped of godz

culture worldview & geography

history became a piece of fire

weighing more than it meant

in the land of locusts

writ in running ink

the testament

tested on the backs

on which it rested

unrepentant sins

confessed by invested priests

rewritten by academics

exploited by bankers

polytricksters

& other stripes of thieves

best go with it down the river

milk & honey on the other side

someone must play cartographer

like clever clarinet

must

sit near the door

know the language

must

leave the signs

blessed & cursed

sacrificed

to sit in the bosom

of unholy snakes united

holding the door ajar

for nappy heretics

to dismantle master's house

from inside the machine

where they grind the bones

of scholars

who are fed lies

to feed to others

yea though they have seen the inside of the valley

they help to manufacture shadow

to get an inside track

to the inside

jockeying for position

praying tenure

dreaming of being

lead sheep

content

to eat well until the slaughter

where they too

are delicious morsels

cuz wolves don't care to know the difference

between the new white & real dark meat

even a cafe au lait with a harvard degree

a card that lets him caddy

skull n bones stylee

is on the buffet

after

selling off

his brothers

that truth in theology preacher

& African nations

to answer

the call

never mind who's on the phone

this is the room

where it happened

happens

the room where

the wheel turns

where they

weighed & sold

your forefathers

the room

your grandparents died to get in

can they see us now

porsches jaguars & triple malts

our metaphoric

tattoo tears

proclaiming

we are abel to be cain

& the sets we used to bless

now mean less than

corner offices & glass covered degrees of separation

from grandma's hands ebonics & collard greens

sometimes it gets hard to remember to remember

playing the insider to outsider game

sitting in the bosom

far from where the hunger lives

walks the street

got a nickname

you forget how easy it is to forget

easier than carrying a banner for an army that got lost

it's warm inside

ain't this where we sent em

integrating them

deeper into the beast

ain't this where we wanted to be

deep in the bosom

ain't this where they aimed us

grands & parents with survival on their breath

bidding us go further

sent us looking for milk & honey

prismatic dreams of integration

rising from the nation

crushed within the nation

why we surprised they forgot to remember

what got wrote down crooked

we were confused

but persistent

in sending them to schools that

taught them to be ashamed of

tales & tongues of fire

invisible stars

country grammar

& the worldview contained there in

along with our most blatant sin

the color of our skin

we done marched & died

trying to find a way into

living like conscripted slaves

intent on arriving

at suspect destinations

hooked on the hooks

from the inside out

trading the smell of pragmatic optimism

for a lobster sandwich

a timeshare on the shore

& college education

for children who don't look like us

success is my tribal scar of separation

from the funk piss & grime

suffocating

the nation

twisted

in the nation

the cost is the death of my negritude

discarded

like a ceremonial garment

which I have risen above

it cost too much to carry

as jackals circle

dreams are drained of liquidity

post-race

seems a good room to stand in

as ghettos are reclaimed by urban explorers

greening occupied territories

without regard for the natives

someday this may weigh more

but if you ain't got an army

it don't matter

teaspoons or pounds it's all the same

they write the code

& sheep they do follow

cuz it's warm inside

best go with it down the river

milk & honey on the other side

someone must

sit near the door

know the language

leave the signs

someone must sacrifice

sit in the bosom

holding the door ajar

for nappy heretics

to dismantle master's house

from inside the machine

where they make their bones

grinding bones

it's hard to remember what you came for

when everything is for sale

& nothing means what you thought it meant

when you began

the distance back to grandma's porch is greater than

geography

& in real reality

you remember

it's not home you're ashamed of

it's you

the runaway

still a slave

resting in the bosom

smelling like milk

manifesting

mama & daddy dreams

of brown babies rising

everybody wanna be somebody

only god can judge me

run your broken tongue

across the scars

become him before

this story

could you carry it

all the dreams

backed up in your bowels

no stage to shine

the joy running out

reality rushing in

the crooked deck

being born with a dead man's hand

a ticket to the merry go round in your pocket

even mama's hand can't

soothe the pain

that pushes out your pores

the road is uphill

covered in broken glass

will someone write

how much it cost

to escape

hide from the whirlwind

to rest in the bosom

smelling of milk

up nights

burning oil turning scripture

while ghosts march

ask colin powell

about the price of sleep

once you cross over

even if you wake up

& come back home to the nightmare

you wrote

ask how much it cost to

pretend you mike

hard as you can

till you think you are

if you can remember

to remember

mama didn't raise no fool
& this weighs more than it used to
could you carry it
if it was invisible
but still bent your forehead to the ground
hurt in your back like old age
from the moment you were born
if it weighed more than you
would you carry it
or fall apart into ragged pieces that smell of
ill-conceived dreams
water colors in a storm
& the wrong conversations

mama said rise

daddy died

sorrow drowning

1000 times in his eyes

dead broken yet alive

a working man

wearing pride like a suit

so you could be you

stand up straight honey

look em in the eyes

do what you need

get inside

the bosom

of the machine

get us some of that milk

honey bring that honey home

we waiting for you to

arrive
who knew
the destination itself
the cruelest cut
most suspect for a boy
whose mama dreamed
a mighty man from the womb
he still the usual suspect
even when he do
what they want him to do
what else can a thinking man do
not to wash away
he is not invisible
can you see him now
with his pockets bulging with
needs & promise
do you see him
reading dred scott & ralph ellison

nobel drew ali & marcus garvey
seeing himself
seeing
how he would make it be
if he could
he has a map
of the road he took
the one that was open
toll free
can you translate
what that cost
do you see him
past looking for the exit
now inside out

can you see him

bleeding in the margins

it used to weigh less

it couldn't have cost more

inked

he had a tattoo tear

it didn't mean now

what it meant then

it weighed less

or more

it was a piece of fire now

it burned beneath his eye

announcing he had been abel

to be cain

the set

emblazoned on his chest

more target than vest

it didn't mean now

what it meant then

it weighed more

or less

then or now

sometimes

it was hard for him

to remember to remember

if there was a difference

his body was a map

he wrote the tale before he lived it

ink told it now after he had carried it

could not put it back where he found it

became it

because

that's how it works

they know you before you speak

if they don't know the code

they translate with their broken tongues

he forgets to care

it used to weigh less

or more

he can't remember

to remember

his body is

a piece of art

telling the story

carrying it

it used to weigh more

sometimes he couldn't care less

how they weigh & measure

teaspoons or pounds

kilograms or life sentences

it's all the same

the tipped scale on his back

held by a blond wearing a blindfold

smoking a blunt

necklace inked on his collarbone

says

"godz grant me the serenity

to hustle on"

r.i.p.'s form both his sleeves

he ain't held his daughter yet

but her name is on his chest

right under

"married to the game for life"

it all used to weigh less

or more

he can't remember which

but he knows they see him

think they know him

he is not invisible

he has a map

the journey

told on his skin

do you see me now

if you do not know the code

your broken tongue

thinks it knows

he remembers not to care here

like no one cared

before he wrote the story

lived the carrying of it

it's his story

it weighs as much

as you choose to understand

he carried the weight of his life

in all his pockets

in his belly

it pushed up into his throat

bled in tattoo tears from his eyes

that weigh more than they used to

he has dressed himself

in tribal scars

his song of being

inked on his body

the book of him

not invisible

"ace of spades"

"187"

a spray of bullets

the number "2 800"

"legendary"

a closed eye on a pyramid

"only god can judge me"

run your broken tongue

across the scars

become him before

the story on his back

could you carry it

all the dreams

backed up in your bowels

no stage to shine on

all your joy running out

untenable reality rushing in

your inheritance

a crooked deck

born with a dead man's hand

a ticket to the merry go round in your pocket

even mama's hand can't

soothe the pain

that pushes out your pores

the road is uphill

covered in broken glass

the destination itself

the cruelest cut

most suspect for a boy

whose mama dreamed

a mighty man from the womb

now he the usual suspect

can't do what they want him to do

trapped in a rebel suit

what else can a thinking man do

mama didn't raise no fool

& this weighs more than it used to

could you carry it

if it was invisible

bent your forehead to the ground

hurt in your back like old age

from the moment you were born

if it weighed more than you

would you carry it

or fall apart into ragged pieces

that smell of

ill-conceived dreams

water colors in a storm

& the wrong conversations

he inked it to his skin

so it would not wash him away

he had to carry it

the book of him

not invisible

can you see him now

his pockets bulging with

needs & promise

do you see him

always a day late

holding up yesterday's coupon

reading dred scott & ralph ellison

noble drew ali & marcus garvey

seeing himself

seeing

how he would make it be

if he could

he has a map

of the road he took

the one that was open

toll free

can you translate

what that cost

do you see him

in the crosshairs

looking for an exit

can you see him

bleeding at the margin

in the dim light of the pale

he has written

the book of him

it used to weigh less

it couldn't have cost more

unsaid

you can't be unsaid

those who attempt

don't got that juice

they try perhaps

but those who try

don't sleep well

they waiting

for the sound of you

remembering they

stay busy

erecting walls

between you &

memory trying to erase

the cause without addressing it

they say your name without

looking at you they

only see what they made

they are afraid of the original

they are afraid of their creation

they would like you

to be quietly malleable

(n)visible so they

pretend not to

see the unassimilated elephant

not to smell the

funky farts

coloring the world but

the funk is real

funky & real

it can't be unsaid

like the undeniable slick

sweet coolness of steel

until it

cuts

shedding blood that

can't be unspilled the song

of language dying can't be

unsung

to survive

it will grab other

words take them hostage

& use them to remember to remember

crossing oceans leaving home

the world turned out like a gourd

no quarter in the storm

being the refugee over & over

in a land you never chose

no harvest though your

blood waters the crops

divided with out you at the table

no shelter from the machine

that wants to eat you

after it squeezes out the

essence of what keeps you

walking upright & still you

at the core when you scratch

past the veneer

smeared to appear invisible

can't smack you if they don't see

you be quiet they listening now

when it all wants to press you down

until you run over your

self on the way to being

what won't drown or wash away

what doesn't burn to carry

what can grow in the

desert

until

unless

you

remember the words

whispered to you before

the light before the air

before you knew the ocean

if you can remember

the words that name your

path they can't be unsaid

you are

unwritten

unless you can write food on a plate

words on paper have little to do

with empty bellies

bloated

as if

hunger were a being

growing

in the vacuum

drawing flies to eyes

puckering brows

painting

something that has no translation in eyes

needs to be felt to overstand

such profanity

has little to do with shades of indigo slanted

or so one would think

words on paper

cannot cut through flesh

sever arteries

causing you to bleed out

in a sandstorm of depleted uranium

that will kill your killers

unconceived children

an irony unwritten

in the law books & treaties deleted from

history manicured to fit

the agenda of the storyteller

not all tragedies are staged for appreciation

some are footnotes in unsung operas

that don't make the page

no manual for humanity

nothing written connects

your brother's homelessness

to the depths of your callousness

no strict correlation

between his lack

& your greed

no concordance

that translates your hunger in soul to

his children's emaciated bodies

in need of milk & human kindness

where is the bible

that starts with an english youth

who learns to

leverage & rationalize

his right to a future

against the existence of the

children of the longhouse

where is the sequel that solves the riddles

plaguing bobby johnson's sons

who after being sold down countless rivers

overstand their desperate need

to decipher

midnight polytrix

the fall of mubarak

& all the faces of gaddafi

along with lies about a post-race era

offered by a café-au-lait harvard boy

wearing a skull & bones tattoo

w/ handcuffs

i am creating a global coloring book

to teach manners to nappy headed heretics

warning them about the danger

of harboring assumptions

that have been spoon fed

& of the folly of

playing with knives

in close quarters & shared circumstance

that cross

borders

cultures

& realities

clashing like zombies in tanks

leaving little room for allegiance

multiplying chaos

in this thin fratricidal air

we sipping

like it's the *final call*

ink

/ink/

writers

blood/indigo sorcery/singing blues &

exaltation/without sound

painted on a page/toneless/pickled

thought/snapshot/no evolution/verbatim

tied/no room for growth/perhaps in reinterpretation/but how

been fixed

tied to a page/inked

like the tangled hearts

under

the spray can clown

tatted on a graffiti artist

ink shall not be moved

/removable only/

with abrasives/scrubbing on skin

/not penciled in/not erasable

permanently marked

inked

set

/as if/

in

/cement/

unmovable

meant to last centuries

semper fidelis

liminal landmarks / shifting geography

nothing means what it meant yesterday

language melts / reassembles

in a different village

wearing a different dress

& goes to market on a different day

/ink/a trick used

to tie lies together/until they weigh as much as truth

/ink/

runs in water

can't change its mind

can be reproduced without a soul

was meant to be fireworks / turned into bombs

ink has often been used as a tool by the devil

stealing/sound

like

kodak stole the souls/of geronimo &

sitting bull/sat them airless/unmoving/safely

on a page/they who ran with the wind/ run no more/nommo

is the wind's return

how do you tie

a drum to a page

/ink/

ain't got no heartbeat

/nommo is the wind/

creation/destruction/life force

crossing the continent

of the mouth/pushing past the borders of the lips/

spit is free/

liquid mercury/can be made to serve circles/or disassemble them/spit

nimbler than ink/can reinvent itself in a raised eyebrow/

sit in the shade of a tone/ can pitch tint/ offer one song/ telling many stories/

far above

empty white pages/spit don't always dress for the occasion/arrives uninvited/

sometimes full of spirits/

is hoarse from testimony/it swears language is its own army

spit

/has lost the land

its libraries stood on/

memorized the words/of books too sacred to write

/ink/

never had the keys to the temple

it always told the story after

unless it was written on the

face of a virgin bride

then it might

tell dreams that signify

maybe

but you got to be sleep to dream

spit is awake

/ink stole/

jazz from coltrane

stole the sound of dance/from delicate dusty dancers/no one wrote about them/

just danced they stories without remembering the calluses on their feet/ink ain't
free/it cost to color improvisation in amateur colors/ while 5 yr olds massacre
100 yr old music/trapped on a page/not meaning what it meant when it was
writ/ink say a lot/that ain't true/some sound fine/some sound like who they
want to be when they mama looking/not the way they treated my mama/not the
way they treating me/not the way they want to treat my kids/my kids/kids &
my kind/ they don't write the color of that down/they keep that parted/ in
with the notes/thrown out like babies & bathwater/ ink been known to be
scandalous/

/ink/

hunts rabbits w/a canon

best watch out for rabbits

packing heat

armed with a quick tongue

& their own history

twisted in dna

how you burn that

if spit remembers to remember

how you shoot the nose off that

if spit see stars

you need to invent a telescope to find

what else it know

you don't know

listen

& maybe you can write it down

/ink/

is good for that

but it don't swear to tell the truth

it's hard to look in the eye

& don't always signify

what it meant

when it was writ

it don't signify

what if /ink/ leave you out/do you still

exist/??/what if ink say you

what you ain't/is you/??/if/ink/ fill the whole page/leaving you only the
margin/do you have room to write/??/if they left parts of you floating in the
ocean/if you left parts behind/discarded out of survival's necessity/do you
write that tale/??/

if you ain't got a language anymore/how you write/??/if they take your
words soon as you say them/??/twist them spin mix them/??/wring profit
from your prophets

??how you

/??/or the story of you

survive

maybe you invent new words

spit in freed styles

wind conjures

never inked

too bold

razor words

meaning changing

before they can write it down

how you like me now

you think you

in the conversation

/??/you think

! it don't signify

like blue black wrinkled old men

in stingy brims

teeth clenching 5 dollar cigars

breath smelling of gin & knowing

from a distance

whose eyes grin

as they eloquently explode

divine curses

like corks from aged wine

you gotta shake ya head

so it don't hit ya

as it moves through the room

strutting like a big butt woman

everybody looking

/??/how you write that down

when spirit rise

round midnight

& can only be appeased

by breath breaking past cracked lips

like wind over sharp mountains

ink can't signify

only chase the wind

nommo is the wind

catching the hems

of old ladies on

sunday mornings

/??/how you write that down

how you write

crossing a desert called an ocean

cosmically homeless

transatlantic transgression

pressed like powder

exploding

purple super beings

the product of projects

overflowing with product

everybody swinging

nobody got time to duck

but we still here

/??/how you write that

/?/what ink know bout real life

without commercials

the artist

the artist/writes/murderous verbalist/

c4 b u cud write/the artist/has moved

/grown/out of chaos/n2 purpose/this

ain't mellowing wine/this hard liquor/it ain't checkers yungsta/

live then holla @ me/battle scars & stripes/ i write/murder

she wrote/w/ea lethal pen stroke/as tears flow/hate 2 kill/but

some shit need 2 die/murder apathy/ignorance/stupidity/waste/

let it go/like a bad lover/let it go/grow n2 purpose/the artist/stronger now/

need is greater now/one word/now/same convo/same problems/same sword/

old soul/seer/deep listener/speaking to the dead/speaking for the dead/

memory keeper/story teller/word to reality/word/stories for sale/for free/for

liberation/for liberating/for liberty/free/for freedom/free to be freed/the artist/run

away slave w/ a pen/w/stories for livin/hexin/holdin us in the circle/to feed us/i

got bricks/tryin 2 build sumpthin /tryin move sumpthin/ swang pendulum swang/

the artist/wading through the funk/ cuz the funk know/ funk know what the dust

don't/funk don't die/ it moved underground/ where the artist/ lives/ forgetting to

barely survive/remembering 2 cre8t out of what's been gifted/ make a way w/the

funk/funk knows/the artist forgets to suffer/absorbing the suffering that surrounds/

the artist/in the funk/ground zero/cre8ting/remembering joy n struggle/more paper/
more keystrokes/??/will it free u/it will feed u/an army got 2 eat/ buildin sumpthin/i
got bricks/an army got 2 eat/bone yard soldiers hungry/hope is almost gone/what we
eat then/these words could be melted n2 bullets/free ya mind/ya ass will follow/mental
groceries/??/got freedom/i slang/bangin 4 u/blood on the stage/R it don't matter/it
ain't the applause/it's the pause/the look in ur eye when u overstand/when u see/crystal
clear/when it gets plain/& u can't run no mo/moved 2 purpose/when u accept the keys

/that's why the artist bleeds/

lyrical libation/redemption songs/prayers for heretics/in search of the wheel/the artist
/got bricks/tryin 2 build sumpthin/
an army gotta eat
/??/got freedom/
i slang

first language

one dreams in first language
it is the language of prayer
first language is where your
soul lives
where home is
when it's raining
fire it's where we land
after falling through
the ground we grow from
the cathedral that holds
the narrative of being
the song sung by the
world to you in the womb
there will always be things
that can only be said in
first language
like how deep the cut
how far the fall
how high dreams float above
rude reality sometimes
only a paint can
can own
the truth
maybe you can find it in a pastel

drug across smooth black paper
extract it with ink from
well balanced pens
scribbled in the margins of
books
some forge it in
bronze or cast it in iron so
it reaches for the sky
or covers the side of a building
that covered the sun
after eating the trees
or sing it over a beat
older than the need to sing
or spit it to a crowd
over a new beat that
you got to learn how to dance to
maybe syncopate it drop it on
the one make
them want to see the
instrument because theirs don't make that
sound dance it elegantly stretching it
over centuries of pain
bending like trees
after being hit by waves
speak the language
godz spoke to you before
you were formed

prayerfully in all of you
like blessing
like reason
like answers to the question
why we will find you
in your first language bent
before its altar making sacrifice
living the religion of it
living in its sublimity
seeing the world through it
first language is
the language
we were
dreamed in the language
of our light
our redemption
song
the way we talk
to godz

dead poets

some say all great poets are dead
they lie for true poets never die
they say all great poets are dead
i say they lie for poets live in the words
are the breath of godz are the eyes
we close the ears we won't use they
are the soul of the world its heart beating
against the funk our only rhythm in the madness
the truest science we were spoke into being
first there was the word & poets are of the word
we all know that the last will be first & first there
was the word speaking us into being poets don't
die they are ingested quoted sampled remixed
spoken into life again & again poets are alive
in the word they say all great poets are dead
i say they are food they are light they are alive
in every poet who eats & bleeds poems
on crystal stairs bleeding blues drumming like
jazz men hip smooth hopping on riffs like
silver smoke curling from spiffs
inhaling dead poets like fog rising over
oceans transforming them into sunrises
epiphanies & mardi gras parades the dead
are always with us great poets sit between us

& them translating remembering for us
because of us are us straining to know where
the wind comes from & how the ocean remembers
to rise towards the moon great poets don't die no poet
who turned verses into bread would be content to
be merely dead poets are bigger than death they
remain on the page in the ear the heart burning in
the brain real poets whose notes are noted quoted
eaten like meat drank down like wine they live
they are the glow after the hint of the tale you know
but can't tell they say that all great poets are dead
i say they lie real poets never die
they are meat & bread
i have come to serve more

voting : 2016

here

at the front of the line

showed up to make my voice heard

that's what they say

here

to pay for my ticket

to the conversation

to be a part of the public sphere

here

words & names on pages & pages

words & names

bowed low

by the bullshit of polytrix

perplexed by

the amorality of polytrixsters

here

paying for my ticket to the conversation

soundtrack in my ear

"have no fear"

praying tipping points

refusing the lesser of two evils

standing in my light

my truth my real reality

my feet in the ocean

face towards the graveyard

remembering to remember

how I used to believe

here

small brown hand over

black heart my democratic

start dancing to the tune
played by my parents with
my great grandparents' bones
we a bunch of refugees
migrating through the confines
of america dreaming
freedom from blood soaked
narratives that smell of cotton
dead buffalo kentucky bourbon
& fervent wishes
we
were somewhere else

here

living all outside ourselves
trying to survive our skin
sisyphus trying to get in
out of the whirlwind

here

at the crooked table

where democracy ain't saved me

here

shopping for new dealers

got my ticket

with old brown & black ladies

& a few black men

droves of young peacock-haired people

you can never tell what tune

they dance dipped in privilege

oozing here-ness manifesting it

everywhere

rolling back to the slave pens

sometimes beside you

sometimes dividing you

"have no fear"

"have no fear"

they buying guns & ammo

by the barrel

smells of fear

obama's picture over the stage

TIME underneath it

it's been time

was past time when we came

it's time to go again

we been refugees desperate to root

seeds spiraling in the wind

we are diaspora

brave & tragic

sign of perpetual resistance

here

children playing on the playground

"you play too much,

everybody play too much,

I ain't playin"

here

this used to be a black neighborhood
still here
"have no fear"

here

sad & mad
thinking about the shit we never had
democracy could still free me
"have no fear"
praying tipping points
& what's beyond
whispers say it's all for sale
it's a clown show
today's the parade
got my ticket to the charade
words & names on pages & pages
we dying for change
feel some kind of way

trying to maintain

all i know

it can't stay the same

silence in the face of violence

people sleeping on the street

tents stretch far as eyes can see

walls of garbage

this won't be my great grands' harvest

we been refugees

running

praying

voting to get free

moving for opportunity

marching because of injustice

standing up even when it was just us

knowing this is beyond us

we pray for tipping points

if it's time

bring it on

there are no more words

in this poem

ready

here

face towards the graveyard
feet in the ocean

here

neither wolf nor sheep

prophets are often thrown into the lion's den

not knowing true lions are friends

to guerillas in your midst

seeking higher paths

upholding righteousness

invested in the movement

of the pendulum

the moral arc

go ask daniel

go ask wolfhawkjaguar

come ask me

king said he believed the arc

leaned towards good

then they murdered king

before robert chrisman died
he said the arc is always
moving tugged one way
then another

i have said its direction
depends on the works of human
hands

those willing to
see & out
naked emperors
wolves in sheep's clothing
pimps & polytrixsters
lined up to bleed the sheep

the arc & its direction
an eternal battleground
where potential wages war
with what is
what has been

carving room for what needs

to be & those who would birth

paradigms

this battle resists

being wolf or sheep

you will be known by the works

of your hands idle hands will

be judged by the reality they

allow to be created

we are all there is

we are the pendulum

we are

breath of the wind

when it swings

swing batter swing

we are

the dull-sounding

thud of finality

when it lands

like a lead dime on now

i walk the road

after king

after chrisman

after malcolm

i am pragmatically optimistic

like cornel west

i aspire to be a shepherd

a freedom fighter like robeson

a clear light like belafonte

a gift to struggle like glover

a straight razor like marvin x

a joshua like baraka

neither wolf

nor sheep

a voice clearly heard by both

a clarion calling hands

to the work of moving

the pendulum

neither wolf nor sheep

walking forward

awake in the eye

of the storm

standing on yesterday

holding court for tomorrow

invoking

with the constant

prayer

of moving hands

a birthplace

for a new paradigm

rendition

i grew in the shadows

of tales of her

the shining

mistress with open arms

who crowned the good

on streets of gold

with a chicken in every pot

a job for every man

& no child left behind

the glorious dream

called america

if you are told

you will believe

/?/maybe

you got to love

a good hook

glory glory

bless this country

(that never was &

yet must be, deferred

adrift in politics

waiting for a paradigm

shift)

america shine light

so we may see

how blind justice is

raining only on

poor men's houses

god only loves the

good only answers

the prayers of

those who tithe

in english or perhaps

cash

no idealist here

we must remain practical

measure the weight of

the means after you

achieve the end

we can lie about the past

time only goes forward

(...he said when they

placed the cable in his

hand every thought of

any pleasant thing that

had ever happened to him

disappeared...)

darkness

employed globally

who's the terrorist

performing democracy

in print

practicing

the embodiment of horror

bury land mines in the soil

where cattle once grazed

the dead do not eat meat

sorrow is free

& apparently invisible

/?/ where are the eyes

/?/ where are the ears

/?/ where is Joshua

(...who killed the fourth estate

embedded it with lies

for advertising dollars

monopolizing compromising

the people's right to know...)

learned to pledge my allegiance

small hand over open heart

learned columbus tarzan

john wayne cold war

bomb shelters chemical war

dirty reds gooks wetbacks

before I knew that

they had a name for me too

in america where

the fires of the world

are fanned with flags

killing with culture

where progress can be lethal

materialism causes blindness

too much makes you deaf

patriotism can make you dumb

side effects or main directives

performed like devotions

to tyrants posing as god

(...& depleted uranium is a

weapon that keeps on killing

silently in sand that blows

into noses slides down throats

into bowels exploding into

uteruses killing into the future

bleeding fetuses onto floors in

minnesota better to shoot blanks

murder is murder is murder...)

who will render the criminals

who identify terrorists

while they themselves

in fine-sounding language

distort murder with bunting

& anthems while cemeteries

overflow & morticians grow

fat buy stock in a future

that has no chance

if the present has

no eyes no ears no courage

(...he didn't go into the army

cause he believed the myth I

swallowed he was hooked by

different fish poverty

was his moby dick he was

under obligation to lift the

anchor still hanging from the ship...)

if the world is composed

of words then god has

stopped talking

because the deaf have

only bags of want

they have forgotten

the sound of children

laughing because the

sun is shining

gone is all but

the scent of naked loss

keened in quiet laments

etched by poets

on scraps of longing

they are afraid to read

at coffee houses full

of blind liberals who

are secret republicans

rabid democrats

neo-communists

voting independent

color blind philanthropists

recovering atheists

practicing Buddhists

living green

leaving no footprint

100 percent organic

& deaf & dumb

(...when they put him

in the small cell he

thought they would

realize their mistake

soon & let him go...)

we live lies

enact illusions

we are not safe

we are not free

not even enough

to open our eyes

(...he said

he will never

feel safe again...)

we do not trust

ourselves

we have given away

our courage

our belief in the possibility

the dream was supposed

to mean what we thought it

meant someone raise the flag

& thump a bible here

(...he said he knows something

he wants not to know

he has seen how the lie

is stitched with human

thread he has looked

evil in the eye & seen

its human pulse & he is

afraid forever...)

we keep our eyes closed

re-membering to the

old tunes from gone never

really here just historized

days like recreated/aborted

camelot shot with dreams of

change we are afraid to

make praying messiahs we

will crucify refusing to see

ourselves as murderers

until we are among the

murdered

buried beneath

the rubble of

our blind deafness

without roadmap or beacon

we want change

we won't change

(...he is home from the
cell the gulag the prison
the army the nightmare
of escape has come true
he is home but will
never see the same
he can hear the pain
he can hear the pain
he talks but it's hard
to listen...)

in the distance the
band is playing
& fees are extracted
the future needs
ears today
tomorrow may not
come without eyes today
when bellies need rice

water is being sold

sacred forests are dying

ice caps melting

& capitalism needs

a heart transplant

& all of your blood

so that the grandchildren of

bankers can go to

private schools

(...he walks at night

waiting listening

he can hear the pain

drowning everything

roaring like a thousand

rivers driven by a wanton

wind mumbling in the darkest

part of his bruised soul like

a million angry voices...)

we need to understand

we are the wind

(...he is coming undone
bullets in the chamber
we are not safe
no safety
he can hear the pain
roaring like a thousand rivers...)

we must remember
we must be the river

(..lies parentheses margins
collateral damage in italics
boundaries crossed
he can hear the pain
like strange strained voices in his darkest night...)

/?/where is joshua
where are a million
angry voices

/?/demanding light

we are the missing voices

we are creators of nothing

if we cannot accept the

pain we have allowed

to dance in our name

across the globe

(...he can hear the pain...)

america, america

/?/ where is joshua

who re-members

(...the pain...)

america

/? /who renders thee

june 2011

"missing gil scott-heron"

superman went home
followed by geronimo pratt

tears & struggle
from harlem to tanzania

souls set free from heavy bodies
x's wisdom brightens the midnight sky

in babylon as
we remember sun ra

in the laughter of the living
lupe proves it ain't all a fiasco

gil scott & plato's cave
revolutionary lessons

never televised

but still in syndication

students remember teachers

x @ 67

for muhajir

baba turned 67
his children forgave him
he may eventually forgive himself
bless the demons that chase him

keep him pouring out
long may he flow forth

we were born &
will no doubt die
thirsty

keep him pouring out
long may he flow forth
keep him pouring out

bless his mama

living brightly in his memory

may she forgive him for

ignoring her at least this once

we worthless negroes are blessed

because

he has never left us alone

keep him pouring out

long may he flow forth

keep him pouring out

in his journey from miscreant to itinerant poet

he grew towards mt. thai & wrote maps

so we could follow

"come to the front of the line"

keep him pouring out

long may he flow forth

keep him pouring out

he turned away from feathers

remembered how to talk to cows

learned from falling down

the value of things he never owned

sharpening his pen to sword point

bargained back his soul from the devil

for poems in the name of his grandchildren

as his students watched

they learned to plant seeds

we know you were here

you have carved on souls

in a forest that plants trees as it burns

in life's fire all is clean

all is new again

keep him pouring out

long may he flow forth

keep him pouring out

sun ra never died he ascended

as you have

standing there in the light

sun over your left shoulder

forever in your righted eyes

bless us as we

"come to the front of the line"

to present flowers to the living

keep him pouring out

long may he flow forth

keep him pouring out

that new millennium dime

the dime

that new millennium dime/

this one

a defining dime

like when you look back & see

you/got grown/learned sumpthin/

this one was not hollow/hit like a lead seal/either the beginning

or the end of something/maybe the beginning of the end

/?/ end of what

it didn't smell like an ill wind

/you had to be there

& willing to dig deep/shit got lost

hot buttered soul/the godfather of soul/the queen of soul retha-ree-

ree-retha/ms. abbey

michael moon walked into immortality/prince partied out of time/

luther left our houses

& our home/we lost shit/baraka became

the myth of drumming fingers having written/ moved on/

we lost shit

rights/innocence/the ability to pretend ignorance/

descendants of stolen africans lost centuries of ground

& the house on it

we lost shit

stelly/graham/grant/tucker/martin

/mixon

& many/ many/ more

too many to name & still breathe

the hood is on fire

the cowboys have come to settle the land

in west oakland/south berkeley/east oakland/hunters point

easy access baby

we moved

antioch/

fresno/

sacramento/

out to

bay point/

the police & the army merged

dsa/hsa/fbi/cia/opd/hap/fu

skip to my motha killin lou

shoot you/ ya mama/ & ya baby cousin too/

need a muzzle on the army/on my street/

nasty buiznez this dime

masks off

in the street/

/?/do you hear me now/

talkin to you/ what time do you think it is/ kinda dime

/?/you still here/how long/

ya think it's bad now/

wait till the smoke clears/

should have listened/opened your eyes/now you in the forest

somebody stole the breadcrumbs/& the rose garden closed for good

heavy dime

#allthechangeucanmake

obama

#onedayuwill

hard dime/hit the bottom/keep on conning

wanna rub his head

he just a man

made

the band is playin

we all just dancin

don't hate/he got a big dance floor/don't hate/same dance floor you
been bleedin on/you can hate/but you gonna pay for the wax & the
tap shoes / that's this dime

last breath kinda hustle

watch the lights go out

gotta blame somebody

clean out the safe & give

that harvard nigga the keys

somebody gotta take the fall

poor skip gates kinda dime

#jaileveryotherblackmanusee

if you can't kill em where they stand kinda dime/

heavy/

don't talk/reading this poem might cost you a job dime/

that new milli dime weighs a ton

might drop on you/

made a 5-star general resign/saw something

condoleezza didn't see/or saw past/hell of a dime

bushes/a brother/bombs/bankruptcy/

/where were we/

talkin bout that dime

where prophets' words/ were prophetic

/but only rich folks profited/

true soothsayers remain

invisible/ to the deaf/unheard/ by the blind/marginalized

by the puppeteers/

the wolves/

who watch us sheep/

little need/ we sleep on our feet/

heavy dime/a decade

where decadence & madness/paired/ a lopsided dance/copious

consumption/ chased by need/seeded in the belly/

of those/never meant to have/ever/bitter

roots & poisoned fruit/the gun

is loaded/johnny can't read/but he can shoot

wounded dreams explode/it was uphill both ways/the load was always

heavy/

take em for the funeral plots they brought

the dead don't know

zombie times/hard to tell the dead from the living/standing round

talking bout nuthin

while the forests burn/feed em 3 eyed fish/let em die/free the land/

resettle it/

currency over/flags/culture/ethics/people

world got smaller dime/we can all get it

make you wanna hollar/they watch & put it on the news/shoot up

your funeral dime

heavy/johnny got plymouth rock tied to his neck/he waited too long

to go/

hung around too long/mad sheep dis-ease/we hung around too long

the wolves are laughing &

night

is

still

falling

times of fire

it is a time of fire

an age of rising

like waves on a

black sea we are

the pouring over after

being pressed down witness

fire on the water we are

the lesson of the lynching tree

the answer to cotton

the trespassers of language

undressing the weapons

hidden in ink

we are the dreams

projected from projects

the residual of slave hollas

before the rebellions

we are the pouring over

after pressing down

we have walked

miles in the rain & not

drowned we will light

the sun we come with

fire we are of fire & water

we are closer to the dust

knowing we fall like seeds

we come forth in abundance

thrive in the flicker

of the slimmest chance

we come bearing fire

born in a time where vanity

rules truth tellers are slain

poets are labeled mad & fire

is born tended

carried in bellies

hearts minds souls

hot like fire baby

we don't want new dealers

we want to write a new deal

renegotiate the treaty papers

the terms of engagement

the boundaries of the public

sphere & all thoughts of

manifest destiny

we come with fire

fire heals & destroys baby

we don't want a new dealer

in this time of callous

disregard the unwashed

walk along the river's

edge wrapped in the echo

tapped out on iron

ogun proceeds

shango gathers the rear

the sound conjures

an unslaved ditty

with a freed style

cadence breaking

the air of ignorance

disrupting

sinister off-key songs of

self-divined too big to fail

democratic failures playing

one note

on the backbones

of the oppressed

 wrapped in lawless

law ink weapons

protecting invisible war criminals

above

law stealing lying dirty hands

operation stealth

cloaked in subliminal

sound bites selling us crazy

at market rate

talking heads full of schemes

no quarter offered

none asked

we have come with fire baby

to light paper houses

deconstructing language

writing the narrative of

rebellion burning with forward

motion on our breath

prayer is better than sleep

action more divine than prayer

movement is life we moving

proof of life baby

on fire with no more

time to dance you a jig

juggle two realities

pretend like you make sense

truth is a sword we got

one reality we refuse to

be crazy for you

might be a good time

for you to stop pretending

like you crazy too truth

is a sword cutting through

concocted innocence

perceived fragility

& delusions of supremacy

one reality

not invisible

carrying fire

forward motion on

our breath armed

with fire & truth

hot like fire baby

dirt

the people

/slowly returning/to the land/

slowly/

slow food

/looking for sustenance in the sustainable

green ways/leaning on unknowing/relearning/undoing

re/remembering what we never should have forgotten/

from dust to dust/how we forget that/two-thirds water/how

we forget that/god alchemy/mimic nature/

god's law is nature/dust know

how we forget

from dust to dust

we are dirt & water

stardust & god's tears

how we forget

the dust know

star dust & tears

how we forget

lookin for heaven/killin it daily/

lookin for god/a billion miles away/

from the concrete sea/ away from the neon sky/

if you can't find her face ask yourself why/&

turn back/ don't trust the left or the right/turn

back/jesus turned water to wine/sand to dust might

be the trick this time/pull a lazarus for all of us/

make us one-half as smart as god made dust/

how could we forget

star dust & tears/ the arrogance of mis- spent

centuries/ against a few million years/we just

star dust & tears/sun sets/ moons rise/rituals

of star dust & tears aside/

nature will abide

sun sets/ moons rise/we were never meant/

to sell dirt or water/mimic nature & we don't need

antibiotics/dust to dust/slowly/ finding sustenance in the sustainable/

no garbage cans/ a one tree kind of world/green for real/back to/

all you got is what your hands make/suns set/monsanto didn't

mimic/

stole & sold/fast majick/sleight of consciousness/the sun will set/

cloned

sheep/frankenbeef/slow cancer/for everybody/live long enough

murmured

the pathologist/we are the cancer moaned the mage/stardust & tears/

in

desperate need

of unlearning/

turning/leaping backwards

don't trust/

the left or the right

/mimic nature/slow down

/turn/revere/emulate/

god alchemy/

nature/the only

law/blueprint for the living/

dust to dust/

sunset & moonrise

plagues are cured by plague

nature abides

always & forever

god alchemy

the only law

how we forget

to remember

the people pt. 1

for the people/

we the people/the people/ tied to the land/ dust to dust/ born in hope/ better

tomorrows/ long days/ long nights/better tomorrows/we

work/ we pray/ dreaming of better tomorrows/ the people/

unaware of the wheel/ the people asleep at the wheel/ the people asleep/

we the people/ following/ planting/ marching/ loving/ bearing/ harvesting/

sowing/stumbling/falling/reaping/ surviving/in spite of ourselves/the people/

who follow/

the sun/

the son/

the surf/

the seasons/

the stars/

/signs

/traditions

/myths

charlatans/

/our fear

the people/ in darkness/ seeking knowing/ dust

don't know/ knows/

sweat/

/pain

hunger/

yearning/for a song/words & tune forgotten/b4 dust is dust/dust wants to

know/why/why dust to dust/why life/why/the people divided/

why/

born of woman/

born to die/why

same as cacti & roses/

no different/

what kills one kills both/ the same

same needs/better tomorrows/more sun/more rain/

we/the people/plagued by nature/typhoons

of greed/the need for better tomorrows/

/searching

/seeking

/destroying

/plundering

/altering

civilizations/continents/cultures/religions/nature/plaguing nature/

plaguing each other

/un aware of the wheel/the people asleep at the wheel/

people who bow to gods/praying in ten thousand tongues/

r u better than yr gods/?/do they kill & plunder too/do they defy & defile

nature/

/?/r they asleep at the wheel/we the people kill r gods/make monsters/steal

in the name

dead gods we refuse to follow/we the people/unmake/remake/asleep at the

wheel/marching w/wolves/thinking like

sheep/we sleep/we the people/quiet fodder/forget quickly/want to believe/

dust don't know/ asleep at the wheel/dreaming of better tomorrow/we the

people pushed to the edge/a footnote in a wolf fight

/asleep at the wheel

the people pt. 2

we the people/

/?/ who/us/me & u/

the wolves work for us/read the constitution/not a good read

but it sold well/

in our name/we the people/don't care how u got here/we the people

payin the cost/of the wolves/who boss the boss/we/the people/own this shit

/?/how you let the butler put you on a budget/flipped script

free range conscripts/shipped off to kill/for better tomorrows/patriots

who won't read the constitution/not a good read/but it sold well/we

ain't who we say we are/we lie/we cheat/lack grace/we got big feet/eco
stepping & polluting cross borders/sell em clean water/say you free/just
don't disagree/free speech/just no hard truths/turn your head/muzzle your
mouth/don't see/pay

/the fee

tithe/

tax/

cost/to be bossed/by wolves/we the people

ain't no streets paved w/gold here/steroids in the milk/?/what the hell
happened to the honey bees & the american farmer/corporate ownership
of your shit/

/?/we the people/what happened/
/?/asleep at the wheel
dinner napkin turned paper towel/we the people

dying of hunger/in the home of the free/where you are free
to freeze on the streets/
home of the brave/incarcerate more people than any other
free nation/war around the

world/hands in many pies/death in the drugstore/in the supermarket/
drugs in the water/lead on the playground/open a prison/close a school/
we the people/asleep at the wheel/

old people eat dog food/ no one can afford medicine/?/how bread cost 5
dollars a loaf/we the people/?/what happened/asleep at the wheel/

therapist chide clients who live off 800 a month over survival sex/ obsessed
with sex /gay rights/right to life/life on the street/bank own all the houses/
jobs overseas/need a degree/school closed/fees up/rent too damn high/2000
a month to live by a trailer park/in the hood/asleep at the wheel/will kill for
an education/a house/a sliver of the American dream/we the people/
asleep at the wheel/we ain't who we say we are

155

we the people/pay charlatans to mind the store/we bankrupt/got caught with our hands in our pants/wolves took the day & sold it back on a margin/we the people/made in the usa/known for pandering shiny shit/ apathy/tv to keep you sleep at the wheel/wolves driving/car full of sheep/ the new white meat/sharks gotta eat/sheep don't count/we the people/ muted/unplugged/distracted by survival/praying/afraid of the dark we cosigned/down to our last dime/who we gonna call/no innocence/just innocents/ waiting/ on we the people/bout to be run over by the wheel/ sacrificed to wolves/w no flags/ pockets stuffed with currency/no loyalty/ they put god on the money/?/see what they pray to/ in our name/we the people/ain't got no money/we the people/in our name/ graveyards fill as bellies empty/in our name/we the people /?/what happened/bloated bureaucracies eating our tomorrows & shitting on today/

we the people

/silent/

asleep at the wheel/

wolves driving the car/car full of sheep/

we the people

the people pt. 3

the people/we the people/my people

asleep at the wheel/ in the trunk of the car/

wolves driving the car/

/car full of sheep/

asleep/

my people/ sleeping on the bottom/bottom of the boat/sleeping on the

ocean floor/my people

laboring

/to survive/

laboring

/in rebirth/

laboring/building gardens for others/laboring

clearing/cleaning/tending/bending/unsoothed soothers/without refuge/

laboring/

my people/building wealth for others/laboring

the bones & blood at the foundation/the mortar

/the stone the builder rejected/thus the foundation is defective/my people

laboring/building a circle/they remain outside/laboring/

singing in a different tongue/growing in adversity

/inverted/rebirthing/a way out of no way/my people/refusing to perish

my people/laboring/an army asleep/birthing itself/laboring to survive

kidnap/genocide/mindwash/genocide/assimilation/genocide/genocide

served with a side of gin & a bag of desire/my people/seeking better

tomorrows

laboring

/to survive today/

/my people/

the wheel is broken

/my people/

the wheel is broken

/sumbody gotta fix the wheel/

my people/needing

clear direction/more gumption/more grit/ a war chant/ an old dance/a
million tongues/clear vision in the static/bull shit detectors/a prime
directive/to embrace each other/to remember/one tribe here/one tribe/
needing/a million hands/one voice/a million feet/one voice/to beat the
drum/remind the pendulum it's time to go/my people/go/one voice/
sounding like Shango/ battle cry/ one voice/ what we do w/freedom/?/what
freedom/?/asleep at the wheel/segregation might have been freedom/asleep
at the wheel/integration coulda been reverse penicillin/ you well/?/how
civil is it to fight for rights/?/my people/turned left/maybe/ shoulda/ went

right to the throat of the matter/ my people/ trustin kidnapping wolves/
to save them/ from the trap the wolves set/ for them/asleep/on the merry
go round/sales/bail/cases/easy guns/easy drugs/gas station food/more jail than
school/robbery/treatin each other like property/killin me/sumtimes
not so softly/shootin one another/revolution reduced to lootin/my people/
Fanon speak to us/help me cure stockholm syndrome/my people/
asleep/wheel broke/wolves driving /car full of sheep/my people/bound by want
there is no milk & honey/that lie was written on your bowed back/bound
by want/

want to be like mike/mike sick/bound by want

want to be down/ bound by want

wanna forget/ridin in the trunk/wolves driving the car/car full of sheep/

bound

/by want

/my people asleep/

domesticated/

invested in their oppression/trying to be like mike/we like what he like/

/?/amos & andy me/see me buck & wing/!/shake that thing/yaassssah/
bought stock on wall street/where the slave pens used to be/good enough
for mike/?/good enough for me/

we free

/to be slave catchers/free to believe we free/
stop looking for freedom/drink the damn Kool aid/

ya free

/free to surrender/cross borders & kill on order/ ya free to kill each other/sell
dope to ya mother/abandon ya kids/ya know how ya live/tickets for the merry
go round are free/funded by the wolves/ya free to ride/free to die/
free to drink chemical alcohol/made it fa ya/newport/?/take two/got some
extra longs for you/inhale the dream/made ya some shiny worthless shit/
go out & kill to get it/wolves wanna see ya with it/ya free/consume the red
velvet lies/it's just a boat ride/free to forget/who pushed who first/free ya
self from memory/forget american apartheid/ya free to forget fighting for
human rights & ya free to keep fightin each other on Saturday nights/free

my people/

searching for keys/keys to survival/ keys to tomorrow/trying find the
wheel/my people/in search of destiny/a new tribe/north american african/
my people/in rebirth/looking for leaders/every woman/child & man need
to be central command/need a sign/be the sign/the light is green/

quit waiting to go/go

my people waiting/

waiting to go/gone fishing/hooked on the hooks/polytrickin & prayin/
marchin to nowhere/locked up/locked out/ on lock/locked down/waiting/
for the hearin/the sentencing/the release date/in line to get a ticket for
the merry go round/my people/ keep bringin knives to gun fights/trapped
in a crooked house/scared to turn out the lights/my people/lookin for
the wheel/knowin it's round midnight/dark enough to wish for daylight/
everything given ain't what it seem/

/everything will not be given/
some things require a fight/can't
hang with hawks/serve the tea party/feed wolves/
refuse the ride/car full of sleepin sheep/

wolves driving/don't matter if the trunk is lined in red velvet/it's the
trunk/& you ain't mike/& them sheep are gettin fleeced/

the wheel is broken/defective foundation
the game is rigged/the house is crooked
/?/how you right a foundation

you can't win a crooked game even if they let you deal/tell the president/

he might have wooden nickels too/wolves driving the car/ask him how you
right a foundation

/the house is crooked/

we don't need a new deal

/we need a new game

/the wheel is broke/

gotta fix the wheel/

wheel broke/

/gotta fix the wheel/

my people

/wolves driving/car full of sheep/

sheep sleep

gotta fix the wheel

them people

/they don't really care about us/

who

/them people/

who

/them people that did it/them people that didn't do nothin/them people
who made it happen/let it happen/them/those people/not us people/other
people/them people/who ruined it/wasted it/broke it/peed on it/them/
those folks/not us/them/the other/not us people/they did it/they caused it/
they made it/they brought it to the table/tied it to the wheel/them people
with the bullshit/packaging it/slangin it/buying it/accepting it/them
people/them dumb people/the ones that don't know no better/we need to
teach em/them people/the bad ones/without god/heathen people/them/
the they folks/ya heard what they say bout them/them people/that craft
the evil/them people who ignore the shadows/the cracks/the lies/the sins/
them/the sheep people/the wolf people/the people who see & don't say/
the people who hear & won't know/the knowers who lie/the people who
continue/knowing the wheel is broke/them/all us/them/we them/we are
they/they are us/we them people/

are we who we want to be

them wheel

the circle/perfect expression/one/isness/reality check/one/circle/perfect/
round as a state of being/full/circle/wheel/forward/faster circles/bigger/
motion/in motion/expression of overstanding/we stood/walked/talked/&
discovered the perfection of the circle/together in the dark/the wheel an
expression of overstanding/one tribe/in a circle/wolves outside/inside the
circle/food/fire/song/overstanding/overstanding the divinity of oneness/
in overstanding we wanted more/bigger circles/bigger wheels/wheel got
too big/who can drive this wheel/somebody got to drive the wheel/take
us where we want to go/greater overstanding/better tomorrows/pave the
road/wheel can move faster/clear the forest/wheel can move faster/take us
where we want to go/better tomorrows/greater understandings/somebody
drive the wheel/build temples to hold our overstanding/bubbling over
breaking the circle/somebody drive the wheel/build us some fences/hold
the overstanding/keep out those who don't understand how we overstand/
we on our way/build a better wheel/flying wheels/driving wheels/sailing
wheels/wheels that turn on money/bigger wheels/who can drive the wheel/
need a big wheel to drive the wheel/drive over the circle looking for bigger
wheels to drive the wheel/how did the wolves get into the circle/somebody got
to drive the wheel/bigger tomorrows/better overstandings/wolves at
the wheel/somebody gotta to drive the wheel/who let the wolves into the
circle/how wolves get the wheel/wolves driving the car/car full of sheep/
asleep/we them people/

asleep

i

i
am the she
& she's the builder
reformed
once lost/now seeking found/

i say don't scratch too deep/you might be frightened by what you see/i
see forever/it makes me cry/i remember to try/i been known to stumble/i seen
i fall/i found clarity in the valley/out of the shadow/i make light/out
of wrongs i fashion rites/to help i get right/stay right/be right/i remember
grind to shine/diamonds admire pressure/became willow long ago/oak
woulda broke/i know/i am not afraid to know/i carry the burden/like a
gift/i know/i see/the path is clear/i listen close/i hear/i remember not to
forget/somebody must tell the story/ some tongue must testify/i carry the
words/the burden is a gift/i say/& may we all be moved/the foundation is
crooked/i offer ground to stand on/consecrated by the blood of ancestors/ i
walk my talk/better to firm the ground/i have considered the ground/a path
in the darkness/voices from the ocean/unmarked graves/the graveyard of
the sorrowland/the walking dead talk to me/the dust whispers/& i listen/
unafraid/ remembering/that i can only know what the dust know/i listen/i
see/i say/canary me/singing/one word/go/i see forever & i cry/i smell
storm/i want an ark/i wonder if we know who we are/i wonder why we
wait/i wonder/i see/i hear & i wonder/about absolute truth/right & wrong/
perspective/other people's gardens/burdens/the sins of fathers/

future children/the future/i hear thunder in the distance/i wonder bout roads not taken/the loves i forsook/if i can die of heartbreak/if there's time to fix all the mistakes/time for another take/i wonder/while i remember/now is all there is/so i keep dancing/trying get it how i live/giving it all/ i got/admitting it cost a lot/i keep on dancing/i am of fire/i am not done burning/out of shadow/creating/roadmaps w/o detours to the merry go round/endless problems /i count blessings/they are infinite/i started before i began/i will go on after i am done/i flow on that ocean/yes/i am what i was told to be/i listen/i am blessed & burdened/i carry the words/i would be food/feeding an army of seers who know & ain't afraid of knowing/i tend the boneyard/crafting /?/signs of life/ready to go

i already gone

money

/money/

man-made/not god-given/god gives/man sells/

can't own nothing/didn't bring nothing with him/can't take nothing with

him/

god gave

god gave nature

/nature gives

/man sells/can't take nothing with him/not even the money/man-made/

you only take what you brought/

can't take the things you bought/

remember the needle's eye

/money/

you can put god name on it

he still don't want it

/he own everything/

he don't need/man needs/god gives/man sells/

dreams/sweat of his brow/dignity/

creativity/inventiveness/science/medicine/water/earth/minerals/

shiny shit

/ideas/fear/ideology/religion/justice/freedom/security/

fees

taxes/tithes

you can't give god money

who you tithing to

/give god your heart

/your time/your faith/your hands/

do not send money

god don't want it

god gave you hands

build him something

you can start with

a better today

feed somebody

give somebody god gives

/man sells

/man needs/

man buys

/money/

an illusion

worth what you think it's worth

/like shiny shit/

better to have power

power can turn money into seashells

beach littered with euros & dollars

/time you find out there ain't no seashells to be found/

ask a conquered government

god gave you power/?/did you sell it/?/sell it for rent money/

/?/trade it for shiny shit

god gives

gave you eyes to see

/?/how much is smoke worth/ask the dust

the dust won't tell you/

ain't no garbage cans on earth/

man sells/shiny shit/& the space to throw it away/build condominiums
on waste/filling the land god gave with what man sells/money/
a curse/ visited by the greedy

those with a love of fences/sold by the foot

to fence/what god gave/man sold/

don't own nothin

musta stole from god

god gave

owns all

needs nothin

man needs

be godlike/give/

be godfilled/give

give like god

/man sells

things that end up in the garbage

waste what god gave

/man needs/

god gives

/gave everything a place/

how things get so out of place

who reordered what god ordered

money/

got a mind of its own/it don't mind the fact you don't matter/money is
mind over matter/you ain't got none it don't mind/ & you don't matter/

money

ain't got a flag/can afford to be disloyal/only clings to itself

/creates lack/

creates want/

creates rocks to crash on

it don't exist/is a trick/

commodifies everything

is only worth what you think it is

like/diamonds/fur/cars/flat screens/property in gentrified neighborhoods/

only worth what you are willing to pay

pay to play lives

/money did that/

we used to make things

we used to grow things

they patented nature/fruit won't grow fruit/money will/ask the farmers

god gave us seeds

/now we buy/

man-made cloned nature

water polluted to make things to sell

/sell clean water/

god gave rain

/man sells water/

we buy

money rules

wooden nickels & dirty paper

makes swallowers out of dreamers

/condoms swollen with heroin/cocaine/death in a bag/dreaming of better
tomorrows/as balloon payments loom on ruptured horizons/overdosing on
need/want is like poison in the belly/bleeding out today

/for the love of money/

we sell today

looking for tomorrow

we buy dreams/& only want brand names

no more homemade

we want whips & chains

/ bling blinded/

man needs

god gave

/man sells/

we buy

/?/can we buy back our humanity

dreams

the dead visit often/i no longer fear them/some i know at once/even if i

never knew them

/others introduce themselves/

they bring things/

riddles/secrets/dreams of fire/memories/instructions/prophecy & the keys/
they warn/they rail & rant at the bedside/they wander through the house/
some speak chattily/others are silent/i hear & understand them all/some
are relatives/sometimes they are other people's relatives/others are heroes
dead & gone/they are all warriors/ once of fire burning bright/now waiting
to rise/we drink & think upon them/

'til they rise again/

geronimo came last night/he was alone

/sometimes he is with cochise/cochise tells

tales of mangas coloradas/long may his spirit live/fallen warrior/

we drink & think

upon them/'til they rise again/perhaps mangas himself will come one day/

/once free as wind/now riding on it/dust in

dreams/speaking to the listening/

last night

geronimo was sitting by the bedroom window/

often he does not speak/there is

little need/it seems i know/what he know/& he know/what i know/

sometimes we watch the fig tree/as according to the season/ it dresses or

undresses/it is

undressing/he sat

& watched it

in its bareness/it unmoving in a silvery silent rain/neath

a waning

moon/

i rose to sit beside him/no need to speak/he know what i know/we both
know/no good comes of wolves at the wheel/i know what he know/blood
on the path/blood on the moon/blood on closed doors/blood at the
foundation/to undo it may take more/

we know blood/

he told me his true name/geronimo is a prayer name/they were praying
when they named him after the saint/jerome/

to no avail/saint jerome did not answer/

goyaałé spoke for him/

we know blood/

mixed in times of war/we know blood/growing in resistance together/we

know blood/

we watch

the tree/seasons change/blood & struggle remain/

/we are instructed by the dust/

we watch the tree/day rises/we both dreamed of zulus

samurais

sharpshooters

& dervishes

/the night before/

a gathering/& sounds of war/

we have heard the howl of crazy horse/in a not so distant distance/

we have talked for hours without words/we agree john brown

was a good white man/

we are uncertain about the existence of others/

we are uncertain about existence

we wait visits from nat & harriet with news of marcus/

marley came once/we were too

gloomy for him/he helped us sharpen arrows & departed/

we watch the tree/wanting to know what it know/waiting for

instructions from the dust/

blood & struggle remain

on mamas

/?/what you gon do with mama

/?/what she do with you

/wiped your nose & ass/

now you mad

/won't be long before you gonna need your ass wiped again/

/?/what you teachin ya kids

/?/what you gon do with mama

/what they gon do w/you/

granny was mean sometimes/so what/life had been mean/
now it was running out/like dead husbands/ & the ungrateful
daughter/w/ that tribe of grandchildren/caught in the
middle of the mother/daughter

divide/

/?/why the hell would she be nice/after that/then/while the pain sang
constantly off key/& constant/like a lover who stayed past the loving
leaving/constant companion to years of memories/not all good/some
wonderful but far away/some bitter as unpeeled persimmon / you want
nice/dying is not nice/living was hard/& the end was crushing slowly all

dreams ever dared/grace stayed in the hallway/afraid to enter the room/
hope had fled/gravity sat by the bedside/holding cold hands/with/colder
hand/?/why would she be nice/having given all/receiving so little/poor
return/she would cuss you for the folks who were not there/as you stood
there/ waiting on her/waiting for her/waiting/she giver of hugs/milk &
cookies/the best sweet potato pie/so small/so much pain you could smell
it in the room/on her clothes/on your hands on the drive home/she was
granny of a thousand smiles/she had forgotten how to smile/she spoke to
dead folks/called you by your mother's name/& she cried/in pain/in grief/for
leaving/she would accuse you of stealing/& you had/not money/but
love beyond measure/all that sweet/sweet love/you took/& took

/what you gon do with mama/?/what they gon do with you/

/?/throw out your life/?/sit it on the sidewalk/throw out your love letters/
photographs/sell your trinkets/give them away/let the trashman take em/
fight over/things/while they cry over your body/what

/?/you gon teach ya kids

/?/what you gon do with mama/with her correcting tongue/
her sharp eye/seeing you/saving you/reminding you/she raised you better/
expects something/

/?what you gon do with mama/

/?/you gon wait till she dead

to succeed/to wake up/to grow up/to show up/to bring her flowers/to love
her like she loved u/ with no conditions/how long before you get it/ when
she blew up/when she showed up/when she didn't show up/when she came
looking for you/when she hugged you so hard you thought you would
break/when she gave you her last/when she borrowed/went without to give
you/& how it hurt her/when she didn't have it to give/

/?/what you gon do with mama

children

they say children are the future/

if there is a future

it should be guarded by your children

/for their children/

children as guardians/future children/

children must stand on the past/protect/revere/change it/destroy it/
rearrange it/obliterate it/but you must stand on it/perhaps in spite of /
or/ because of it/but/ you must remember/you must

realize/there are no wheels in need of creation/we just need new paths
to roll on/you will not create revolution/?/will you move the pendulum

/?/will you light the fuse

don't question the bridge you came across/rebuild it if its faulty/
never fear rebelling against it/build on top of it/but don't forget what
the foundation of this moment is/

draw from it/

/paint a future your children can rearrange

/if you need to be cut/to learn knives are sharp/you

will waste a lot of time bleeding/

time

is funny/the road

looks longer than it is/

dance quickly/burn brightly/dream loudly/now

tomorrow is not promised/grow

old/

become

your parents/only better

fix it/

don't forget what you know when you come here/remember

/the gift you were told to share/remember

close your eyes/remember/don't forget/imagine/open your eyes

create/see/be

truth

is your friend/truth is heavy/ you are strong/let's pretend leads to let's do

/do/

stand on the ground/sink in roots/spread your arms/open your mind/now fly/

there are no limits

/just unknown wonders/wonder

/dare/ make/ run/ fall/

cry/

run again/

again/

do it again

woman

it don't mean nuthin

without a woman

don't mean nuthin

god wrapped velvet/over tempered steel

& made a woman/in the image of the creator

/creators of life/

godly metaphors/virgin mothers

mothers of godz/or/monster makers

/creators/

/deep water magic/

we need new mirrors/to see ourselves as we are/to reflect us as we were meant

to be

bring me the moon/I want to see myself

full/w/o the basket of burdens

weighing me to the ground/where is the moon

if i could weave the tears/i would cover the scars/i would turn the sound
of women crying into laughter/& the smell of sunshine/i would make
weapons of the anguish in our eyes/when we think of men & children/
i would give jeweled armor to the yearning/for home/where things grow/

children/relationships/flowers/dreams of tomorrows/tomorrows

we are curved like African drums/soft as drugstore cotton/strong
as moonshine/memorable melodies/rolling like ocean/
haunting/inspiring/nourishing

some are husks/sucked out/see the bitter bitch/once queen/once princess/
baby/honey/sugar/darling/

/closed

gone

lights out/

steeped in bitterness/smells like regret/loss/emptiness/sour hope/bruised
love/broken promises/too many chances/burns like acid/

/?/who would piss on flowers

we are not disposable/not interchangeable/not throw away/do not play pursue
& abuse/don't hit cuss/kick /neglect her

/?/who put her in the dumpster/left her half-naked on the side of the road/
raped her/?/raped & beat her/?/raped beat & killed her
/?/who sold her body like lumber/?/who used her until she was a dust-filled

husk/no sparkle/no bounce/no music in her laugh/no flower smell/
no silk swish/no gentle clang of golden bangles/no perfumed hair/no
pomegranate lips/no rose petal hands/

/?/who made her a video vixen

just a body/might as well be a machine w/tits & ass/shake it mama/
shake it like dice/drop it now/snake eyes on ya/pull it up/pull it down/
bend over/shake/?/who reduced her to a mouth & pussy/who reduced her/
whose ho is this

who gave her a gun & told her/now you equal

/? /who said use what ya mama gave you

/?/what ya want ya mama/daughter/niece/sister/sweet little baby girl

/to do for that slick cat/think a little sumpthin like you/

/?/what you want mama to do

/it's a man's world/don't mean nuthin/nuthin/

/?/where's the room for wounded women

wounded in the hands of lovers & friends/twisted/twerked/
worked/pimped out/touched too soon/not touched at all/needing touching//
broke like a scratched disc/no music playing/long gone/
just hanging now/dead on the inside

185

/i want to be an ocean woman/

life giver/soft yielding/firm shores/sun rising/moon glow/magnolia
scented/juicy peach/perfect storm/hibiscus honey flavored/have you
seen her/ain't no woman like…/a love song/sought after/held like money/
open as a meadow/wonder woman/revered/touch me in the morning/a first
& last thought/an obsessive addiction/deep desire/fetish/hold me like
you loved me before you knew me/sing in my ear/give me all you got/&
want me to have more/adore me/know me & love me/still/let me be
that woman/start your heart/stop you in your tracks/make you want
to be correct/let me/touch your soul/soothe your body/ease your mind/
be east to your west/let me/be that woman/let me

be that woman

brother brother

men wanted/to hold their ground/to keep heads to sky/wanted/in

arms/homes/hearts/lives/wanted/by
their wives/sons/daughters/brothers/nation/block/hood/mothers/fathers/
sisters/wanted/for lifting/carrying/loving/protecting/guidance/counsel/
wanted/for dreaming on/ needed urgently/because

the world needs the image of god/men wanted/made in the image of god
brother brother
head up/be up to it/sky up/god up/
nights are longer here/bring me the sun/light this up/

i speak of kings/known not for the show of wealth/but rich cats/with
heart/known for being a man/hard ground that/but he cover it/invincible/
can't be broken/bury him first/wild flowers will grow where he lies/known
for being a man/not broken/determined/work all day/laugh deep like
thunder clapping/love hard/ain't fraid to cry/over birth/death/& in love/
known for being a man/hard ground/kneel only to pray/willing to be the
last man/raises men/known for being a man/i speak of kings/builders/not
broken/husbands/lovers/fathers/brother.brother

create hope/sometimes that's all there is to eat

still hungry/create more

if you want more than hope/make it

ya been makin it/a way outta nothin/

making it/with the world riding you/making it

shake/rumble & roll/strutting it/two dice & a nickel/

with/only a song/ballin/tryin get on the ball/playin ball/not playin/
just ballin/livin to ball/trynna get the ball/holdin ya balls/protect ya neck/
& ya balls/

sumtimes

seem like that's what you got/balls sans opportunity/brass balls/elephant

balls/?/you still here/ man that's balls/

have the balls to raise your children/that's revolution man

raise your daughters/show them what it means to be treasured/

raise your sons

feed them hope/sometimes that's all there is/

but it taste better than excuses/no money/no job/no ride/its yo mamas
fault/i would have/should have/was sick/too young/too dumb/not ready

get ready/there's a storm coming

/think it's wet now/

a storm is coming

/better build an ark/

better think like noah/think/past today/plan to live tomorrow/plan to live

be a man

/if no one showed you how/be what you missed/be what you need/

be what we need

plan to be/tomorrow is planned today/?/are you ready

ready for a storm/locked in/locked out/out group/outside/inside out

who you gon be to survive/better be like noah/build sumpthin

or get washed away/

feed your family/don't let them starve mentally/?/

what you know to teach them/

ignorance is a storm/your children are hungry/don't let them drown

feed them hope/if they still can't swim/teach em to fish/

become a fisherman

there is a storm coming/are you ready

what if master won't feed you/

/?are you ready/?/what if the slaves are really freed/?/are you ready/

if no lights come on/when bread cost ten dollars/?/

when they wanna sell air/

/?/what you gonna do/when the storm come

/?/is ya ammo dry/dare/nuthin to lose but shackles/

god up

create/you are the cavalry/go

/shape shift/get out the lane/quit the game/it's rigged/ya chips are wooden

try cashing em in/bamboozled

better recognize the truth

/sharpen to a sword & make a point/storm is coming/

stay off the merry go round/tickets to the ship are free/

lock up those who won't play/

the game is crooked/you pay to get in & out/grab ya balls/

this is risky business

i speak of kings/easy boys/ride the ship/incarceration is a plantation/

real world is harder

ask ya son/ in the cell across the tier/whose raising your grandson/

& it don't stop

/?/is your ammo dry/ recognize the truth/sword point it/get free/

make sumpthin/made man

what you make/make sumpthin

we got needs/supply them/

fresh food/clothes/housing/essentials don't change/still sell like crack

/rock up your resolve/be solid

refuse to die for shiny shit/decide what to live for

/decide to live/live & let live/you are ya brother's keeper/feed him/less likely
to rob you/respect him/teach him to respect you/i speak of kings

/?/is your ammo dry

polytricks

nuthin good/can ever come

of a herd of

sheep/following a pack/

of wolves/

the sheep

are deaf/blind/walk in their sleep/

the wolves

are wide awake/ravenous/sharp teeth/mean dogs

known for shittin where they eat/

/who left the wolves to tend the sheep/

wolves say

sheep picked them/

/lions say

the wolves tricked em /ya been bamboozled

/tainted milk/

/laced with poisoned honey/

noses to the grindstone

/the three-card shuffle is on/sell em what's behind door number two

if they buy that shit/sell em this too/

tell em the first ones free/get in line early/for a small fee/

ya get two for the price of three/deluxe luxury

last survivor gets groceries/tomorrow

promise them a tomorrow/they will follow

/we gon work it out

/tomorrow/

for now just follow/don't remove the blindfold/please/

no references to history/

pay no attention to what you think you see/keep your mind in the car/
ignore what you hear/the biggest conspiracy is the conspiracy to convince
you there is no conspiracy/bloodlines/lines of blood/cost a lot to make you
dumb/cheaper to divide ya/fight amongst yourselves/sell ya guns/supply
choices/conclusions/help you draw lines/we got peace keepers/will sell
street sweepers/we got grief givers/& grief relievers/mass deceivers/buy &
sell you/pen stroke ya/veto ya/legislate ya/charge you/define & fine you/
fees please/devine for you/spin you/spin it/spend it/steal it/blame the
wolves/or blame

the believers/

/sheep/

following wolves/nuthin good

can ever come from/

litanies of legal fictions/father knows best

/keeps the truth close to his chest/*they dont really care about us*
content to devour/you & toto too/sneaky sorcerers

/manifestin ya destiny/

cooking books & sound bites/mixing media

/to feed sheep

50 inch flat screens in a soft economy

3d stupidity 24/7 on tv over 5g in 4k

buy what you see/hear/can be made to believe/

the wizard is in/news at 11/

lead story

/wolves save world/super wolves/sheep applaud/continue sleeping/meanwhile

behind /edited/ scenes/

wolves divide world

/sheep sleep on/

wolves on verge of destroying world

/film destroyed/ sleeping sheep destroy walmart on black friday/news at 6

sheep march for immigration rights
/ice raids school/polytricksters make deals on super highway in euros/u.s.
economy plunges/real estate is big in viet nam/iran/iraq/as are war
criminals/buying land/investments in infrastructure/drugs/dope
the conquered/wanna party in dar salaam/wars are real estate forays/
shoplifting excursions/the secret is/ they are society/*they don't really care
about us*/super wolves/super schemes/sleeping sheep/slippery slopes/more
sheep slain/no news/

lead story

/giants win/

national guard on street in oakland for oscar grant rally/no coverage/

marchers riot/ film at 6/ 10/ 11/ & during regular programing/

sheep asleep/casualties high/tree lighting news at 11

father knows best/keeps the truth close to his chest/ain't no profit in peace

sheep are chess pieces/you ain't in the game/you are the game/they preying/
not praying/they the only ones playin/the house is crooked/vote on that/
door is nailed shut/you ain't invited/ if you found the game/ it ain't the
game/you got the wrong chips/wooden chips/try cashing em in/you been
cashed out/yesterday

wait till tomorrow/follow

line up/the lies are free/sign up/serve/join/protect/worship/defend//
keep ya eyes closed/don't peek/the magic works best w/eyes closed/stay
sleep/tomorrow/we will work it out/ tomorrow/smolder in the glitter/splash
in the shards of shattered useless shiny things/more tomorrow/
stay tuned/sales/free fear/sales/more tomorrow/for rent/for sale/lease
cheap/tomorrow/we will work it out/sweet dreams/
it's only a problem if you wake up

race

granny said/

"you will lie in the pit/you dig

for an-other"/

/?/how you sleep

here in the pit/where

we lie/side by side/ in the same open grave/pitted against

one another/ cain & abel forever

/?/how you sleep

/?/has your god been watching

/?/do you pray

with the same mouth/that sucked at

my great great great gramma's bloody tears/hollered

sold american/

nigger/kike/spic/wop/chink/spook/slant/beaner/dego/sand nigger/

camel jockey/

jungle bunny/jig a boo

/?/how you sleep

/?/spooked

do you dream brown hands

wake sweating/vowing

to kill them all/so

you can breathe

with no fear of

retribution/do you dream of severed breast/broken bodies/?/are you

greedy/in your sleep

/? /how you sleep

with your bi-racial grandchildren waiting for your death/the

brown-eyed ones that are ashamed of you/?/how will you answer god/

when he asks you about his children

do you dream burning crosses/bodies flopping behind trucks/
dogs at throats/shooting first & yelling stop over dead bodies/corpses swaying
from trees/the smell of burning genitalia

/?/how you sleep

/?/do you ever fear drowning in oceans/of grief

crafted by you/are you fettered

by your fictions/

/?/what if we are human

/what will your god say/

/?/how you sleep

/?/do your sins trail you like a caravan

of bodies chained to one another/

full coffins/full coffers/

empty souls/

futile lives/

afraid of the dark/more afraid

of the light/forever

fearing the morning after/a single shoe falling

& the sound

of my laughter

/?/ how you sleep

when the chatter

from the boneyard is deafening/

/?/how you sleep

on the edge of an open grave

/?/how you sleep

blue ball

one ocean/one tree/one/you

lookin for water/on the

moon/

mars/but you/ the one

that poisoned the earth/rivers/ fish

in the lake/the

ocean/full of antidepressants/

fantastic/ya dumb ass invented plastic

spray more/harvest more

clone it/they don't need to know

make it from corn/it's all corn & sugar anyway/that's how you feed slaves

better than/ chickens/cows/

just barely/hell

spinach

beef

eggs

lettuce/

can kill you

wax them apples/make em shine

dig here/build there/don't care where the

mountain lions/deers/bears live

shoot em if they show themselves

we are here/3200 sq feet & a view

with a jacuzzi/lovin nature

put them animals in a zoo/noah had a good idea

/tunnel there/dam that/level that/cut it up/dig it up/

build a fence around it/

/when in doubt

kill it/

build parquet floors with those trees/make tennis racquets with the others

clear the forest

drill offshore /forget

marshlands

deltas

acid rain/tsunami/cyclone/hurricane/

quakes/faults/volcano

nature can be a cold bitch/woman scorned syndrome /

humanity as an infestation/that

must be purged/extinguished

like a flame/fire next time/

& then/

perhaps a new ice age/the dust know/but

we forgot

we should

have/not

made more than we could use/take

without replenishing/greedy

ungrateful bastards/better than nature

synthetic/test tube/new/under godz sun /artificial

intelligence/we god mentality/the dust know

/?/but do we/done

did/too much/ask the dust

kill with efficiency/accidentally/ dead is

dead/

the dust know/dead is dead/sun

no ozone dead/ no season species die dead/misdirected

migrations/the bees left/fend

for self/ in the man-made valley

of death/where air

will be sold/before the dust

speaks for all of us/

silent as a dead forest/

one open grave/

ask the dust

war

good for absolutely nuthin

laughing wolves wage war worldwide/the

tears of mothers fill seven seas/seals

have been broken/the veil

is torn/

the dead

may be the lucky ones/night

has farther to fall/before

day breaks/children soldiers/patriot terrorist/

zealots/demagogues/oligarchy/

the fall of eden/& babylon/swallowed

in a cloud of greed/colored bright red by hate

sandwiched sloppily between fear & need/

murderous marches into territories occupied by human lives/

we are master mercenaries/we will kill/

for money/oil/land/diamonds/water/salt/food & housing/education/

benefits/that don't exist on a barren planet/

ask the silent forest in russia about nuclear winter/ask

the coffins in the cemeteries w/tattered flags forlornly fluttering/ask the ghost tied to the mass burial grounds/ask the dust

/ask the dust/

as night falls slowly/over nothing/?/who

will ask

/the dust don't know/

but we should have/

we built bombs that only kill people/industry is sacrosanct/ ask the dust

the dust don't know/

settling softly over all/that could have been/will never be

/not speaking the lies

boardroom deals/war is big business

/ask the orphans/

living in the shadow of reparated opulence in dar salaam/or ask the dust

neither speak/but money do

religious war/warring religiously

ethnic cleansing/ genocide by stealth/bio terrorism in lands where nutricide/
homicide & suicide hold hands/served in a buffet of diseased blankets &
cultural distortion/alcohol/dirty cops/medical experiments/crack/ice/meth
& extra nasty ecstasy w/fentanyl for all/keep you at war w/yourself/lost
soldiers/can't find the battlefield/war with everyone else

war

as population containment/war

as a form of exploration prior to exploitation/ war

a budget balancer for billionaires/war

the dead don't talk/but money do/war

cain slew abel

war

money changers

rich men/threading needle eyes

rent dreams of heaven/to the poor

served with a side of by n by/the meek will inherit

dust

& pay a healthy inheritance tax/ capitalism

eats its young/mucho money for weapons/minds

lie fallow/sow want/reap need/

no house/

no food/

no coat/& baby it's cold out here

no boot straps to pull up/no boots

/no doctors

/no place to grow/

dreams die/starved

& baby it's cold/in a

deficit soul/too poor

to live/but can't afford to die/they took

the land/& those seeds won't reproduce/they took

what was underneath the land/minerals ain't got rights/water ain't free/they took

the air over the land/then they

sent my job to indonesia/can't

afford pride/will work for food/will

work/they murdered detroit/good for ford/good for the usa/

that's what they used to say/

factories closed/don't need your service/industry moved overseas/

don't lie or sit here/gated communities

/locked churches/

closed schools/

hospitals/soup kitchens/

welfare rolls/closed/bankrupt/closed/

foreclosed/fraudulent/money

may be an illusion/but

the need is real/hunger kills

more people than bullets/desperation

loads guns/can't afford to care/ got to survive/buys dog food for dinner/

can't afford medicine/lives in a box by the police station/

can't afford justice/

can't pay for care/distracted by survival/too tired to

resist/no gas money/ no

car/no suit for the interview/no extra/

never enough/need/want/want & need/death

is an exit

/too poor to die/will

work for dignity/no jobs/jobs left/rich got richer

/poor got poorer/too poor to die/we drank the tears/thirsty/

thirsty & hungry/sell em back their own water/hungry

/it's hell here/will work/the bank took the house/

furlough days/ furloughs from pay/

rent too damn high/ lay ya ass down & die/too poor

sell a kidney/a lung/rent your womb/

put tomorrow on layaway

/charge a life/

will work/told us there was milk & honey/will work for either one/

will follow wolves/

will be sheep/

will sin/

to eat/ to pay the mortgage/will work

will kill other hungry sheep/

the night has farther

to fall

before

day breaks

song for dirt & water

this is a song for

dirt & water

star dust & tears

a dark cosmic prayer

for redemption

help us forget

what we never needed to know

someone

beat the drum slowly/find the road

we are ready to go

must there be blood

plagues & war

how much does it cost to ignore

drunken children pissing in the ocean/while nero fiddles

haven't we been here

before

this is a song

for

dirt & water

star dusted complexity & tears

i thought god had given orders

now i can't remember

cause of what he let me see

from chaos flows divine order

this a song

for

dirt & water

ain't we been here before

though we swore we'd never pass this way again

sounds of drums

women crying

the smell of death

greedy men lying

how much is a mountain worth

if it's the only one

someone said suns set

moons rise/ we suffer because we forget

dust to dust

two thirds water

nature's law is divine order

flowing from chaos

godz breath in all of us

holding hands on the precipice

drunk on arrogance

stupid enough to jump

plugged in

gone virtually viral

we order

they deliver

our lives are scars

what if nature decides to heal

this a song for

dirt & water

sing loudly

while we are here

99 swang

99 sheep woke up

/came in from the toxic fields/in search of a song

/full of tick bites

/wolves

against no walls/on a come up/calling bluffs/tea parties full of donkeys &

elephants

99 sheep infiltrated/media affiliated

/99 sheep

awake/from a long slow dance/a tango w/existence

insistent on voicing the relevant/trying to remember the song

/seeking the face of god

/in small foot prints/& elevated empathy

/99 sheep sitting by the last tree/

near a polluted sea/

under a dirt colored sky/listening

for the dust/wanting to know what it know/trying to remember the song/

undoing/unlearning/unwilling to continue under standing/

over standing imminent/not willing to stand under falling skies/

while a woman in white cried

/a poet hypothesized/& the band don't miss a beat

ya know this a dime/see it swang/see it swang

/?/anybody seen my song

/maybe too late/did we stay too long

swang pendulum

/did we stay too long/suns set/

aquarius on the dawn/spring forward for me/spring

unseal fates

the poor are getting poorer/greedy getting greater/

the poor stand in line after line/opening up store doors/

never getting enough/99 sheep want more/see them stomping on

what held them up before/but still can't get enough/

camping on wall street/city plazas & outside retail stores

open—open

we want more

/shiny shit/more lies/more open eyes/more of the sheep to realize

/in real life/the winners live & the losers die

/no one testifies/

watch it swang/watch it swang/?/does the movement mean anything

/or is it just the latest dance/as the sun sets in babylon/

somebody wake nero/tell him it's time to go/

/?/are they selling humanity in the store/will we find it by the fire

as the sun sets/?/will the truth finally feel safe in the open/or remain hidden

behind/the lies /

is there a final truth

/big enough to sing us human/ so far from

the garden/driven by the wheel/ who's driving the wheel/who stole my song/

i know i should be singing/wake me up

99 sheep/still trusting polytricksters/take their ritalin

& march/hoping for brighter tomorrows/should have remembered

we the people/we invented the wheel/we let them drive it/wolves at our table

driving the wheel/99 marching sheep/say they long to be free/

SorrowLand rebellion/

who own this army/who own this revolt/who are these sheep

pharaohs army watches/barely distracted

from setting fires/ burning forest/designer drug & king making/
god build us a better reality/show they just faking/war waging/culture
caging/world carnage/ for cash consumption/dollars over you
management of everything/no social medicine/

let em die

/less of them to kill/lock up/case manage

disconnect/foreclose/evict/leave them without a song/

waiting to go/

/raid/disperse/reassemble/sheep movement/

one planet

/occupado/in search of a song

a place for everything/how things get so out of place/

wolf movement/

/disrupt tyranny/cry the sheep/

stay in ya lane reply the tyrants/

at the end of a paradigm/sheep remembering the wheel

sheep want the wolves out of the circle/wanna slow down the wheel/

want to remember/beginning to want to overstand/what they ought to know/
should never have forgot/dirt & dust lessons/leaping backwards/
with authority/never should have forgot/remembering the days before the
wheel/& the day we let a wolf come to dinner/woke up sheared/fleeced/out to
sea/wrapped in red velvet/surfing the internet/looking for the
wave of tomorrow/they fenced the wild west/young men get on a ship/the
new frontier is the front line/middle east/africa/make us a market/we got
shiny shit for sale/made in indonesia/99 sheep woke up/ & marched/like
shearlings/worried about tomorrow/confused about yesterday/lookin for
the wheel/

got to take it back/

99 sheep finally see/maybe eligible for freedom/singing

want a dialog/turned off the tv/repurposed twitter/

signed out of facebook/went into deep sleeper status/went underground/came

out the closet/

became diverse/longed for polarity

leaderless/leaderfull

messy/like democracy/confused like a slaughter yard

sheep/won't drink the water

turned off the news & became the lead story

/revolution televised/from cairo to oakland/

from the foothills & in the flatlands/fall fell on sheep

springing forward/spring around the world/the day of the lamb/song heard

round the world

lamb rising/SorrowLand rebelling/arrested/encamped/blind folds off/
still marching blind/in need of an endgame/funky/dog shit/hay & tents/
wall street/ogawa plaza/san jose/ berkeley/ sebastopol /boston/denver/
campuses /washington/the state of the states restated/by sheep on a
wolf hunt/no time for a blue-blooded tea party/invitation to rebellion/
SorrowLand rebellion/SorrowLand spring/day of the sheep/ sheep take the
street/but/can they take the day

/?/

dignity ain't free/anarchists/scientologists/bar keepers/ barbers/free
ranging/candle making bakers/technologists/ bee keepers/
buddhist & baptist/organic/green/unemployed/
underrepresented/unarticulated/ disenfranchised/
othered/unimpressed north 'mericans/one paycheck away from it all falling
down/or living in the shadow of their lives /
after it fell down/broke on the hill & crashed into the
abandoned 'merican dream/

wolfs offer permits

/?/how civil can civil unrest be

/tired being run over by the wheel/

would buy american/ain't got no money/

ain't got no job

ain't got no house

ain't nuthin made in 'merica anymore no way

/we export broken dreams

/99 per cent got

broken lives/out of warranty/sold with a balloon payment

/& its past due/

got a lien on it

in danger of repossession

ain't got enough faith to keep dancing/99 sheep

/& the band don't miss a beat/

chronic homeless as a frontline/absurd in america/the displaced embraced

/?/too poor for the 99/wait one more payday/living a foreclosure away/?/

are they crazy before they lose their houses/invisible now/

99 lookin at ya real face/

sheep is sheep

/?/or would you rather be a wolf/tics/against no walls/

ask a veteran how it plays

on a slow day/after your killings done/ya just another one of the 99/

they told us

jesus was with them/in search of the one/but i remember the camel's eye

/& wolves lie/

divine dope/

duplicity/

& sheep/

miles to go/

awake now/don't sleep

dawn might come/revealing/ paradigms broken

like running yolk/thrown off/by sheep standing

/we are the people/hear us singing/we are the people/

brickhouse women

mama

for ernestine

my mama had hands
knock you into next
sunday get you right
quick she knew what
you thought before the
thought formed we were
instructed to think
good thoughts she
was intuitive to
a point she wanted things
she discerned how to get them
she was brave had to be
so she was
bigger than a
survivor she learned to strive
she had secrets some we knew
some we learned others died

with her she was stubborn like that
she had little use for
weakness so we were able
she had been wounded somewhere
but she kept that to herself
it drove her in ways we could not
understand she medicated her demons
but they would howl
& rage at times
she was hungry for life
she had a small slice her dreams
were big enough to hold more
she was wise in her way knowing
enough to get her way her life
taught more than she shared if you
were a part of her she would fight for
you she could let go of things
not the source of her wounds or
the way life made her a warrior woman
don't know if she knew she was born to
the sword & shield but she carried the

banner none the less taught me to go

forward in the storm to make what I need

to trust myself because sometimes that

be your only counsel she taught me to

cover the ground with my shadow

to draw a line you can't cross with your

hands closed she made me who I be

by negation and adaptation I follow her

down paths she cleared I carry her

with me through doors she never opened

into rooms she would have dominated

had she been given what she gave

she is with me in the desert of my despair

she is with me on top of the mountain

many mountains behind us

many more in front of us

ashe mama ashe

look at the view

brick house women

brick house women

don't dream god they

dream of the ocean

walking on water

through fire

of rising

like mist over rivers

overcoming with the sunrise

standing up when the sun sets

when they dream of

falling they then dream

flying without wings

they dream

solutions miracles

with eyes open

pray with

hands moving

only go forward

brick house women

endure

cracks in the wall

water rising

sky falling

the world on fire

they endure

like music

like the smell

of dirt after rain

like flowers

in the desert

they are the foundations

on which we

build

standing after storms

last house on the block

make you wanna

hollar in between

trying to make life

brick houses

built on rocky ground

still standing

brick house women

endure

in praise of memory

i remember to remember

i remember born knowing

i remember knowing

before knowing

i remember

sankofa bird on my doorstep

singing the ocean for me

every step i take

every breath i take

wind & dirt instruct me

i remember the language

it is the language of creation

it is my first language

i remember to know i know

the dead refuse to let me forget

my gifts are their presence

in the present flowing freely

whirling in the whirlwind

making a path for i in the storm

creating vision in the valley of

the blind so space may

be cleared for

the lame to dance the invisible

to be made visible

i remember the reason

for the rhymes the ways

the means out of no way

without means i count

abundance in the valley of

shadow gifted overflowing

prosperity all that's required

of me is stay the path

remember to remember

chart the way

tell the story

trust in the godz

but tie your camel

keep your powder dry

your machetes sharp

hands open

open hearted

one direction

forward

i remember

to bide time

to bank fire

to stoke embers

to cut cleanly

to bleed for myself

that i was born

with dignity & everything

that my path is cleared

that i am blessed

not with perfection

but potential overflowing

running over cups full

no empty plates

praying with hands moving

manifesting what's

been promised at the

end of the day full of

honest labor unafraid of

work i am rewarded

i manifest

clearing roads

like they were cleared for me

i remember to remember

to burn brightly

uphill is a direction

i am here till it's done

i got instructions

i been here before

that's why it looks easy

but it took generations

to stand in self again

seeing clearly the way

the roads been barred

how to jump the hurdles

how to say truth

& maybe live to see the

sun rise knowing is not

just the destination it is

also the journey there

you got

a duty to life

you owe it living

you owe it memory

forgetting is a drug

enjoyed by those who

can afford

not to see the paint

doesn't go up to the ceiling

the emperor is naked

the deadly effects of

invisible nooses over

hidden pits

the smell

of cotton laced with a taste

for sugar wafting in the wake

of chasing empty

things destined for landfills

amnesia is not on the menu

for those anchored to the north

star & dreams of movement

much older than locomotives

not the place of those

in brick houses

with calla lilies growing in

the yard inside filled with

the smell of fried chicken

harboring

hope & fresh fruit

both kept in

brown bags

dream still

i still dream

flying free

i dream the rising

after free-falling

after the ocean

after seasoned

breaking shattered

into a million pieces

blown like dry

thistle into the whirlwind

circling reality not

able to land no

resting place the purge

after the hunger

after the trees grew flesh

silent scream after silent scream

i still dream

in the deep stillness

between breaths

coalesced of what's left

the indelible

the unforgettable

little more than the

sound of the wind

through blood soaked leaves

fed on dreams of dead people

unfulfilled prophecy

unspent potential

wounded but unbroken

i still dream

i still dream

flying free

i dream the rising

after free-falling

holding my breath

hands moving

praying to pass over

answering the call

serving a higher purpose

seeking grace in battle

firmly on the path

machetes sharp

eyes open unafraid

knowing it's always a good day

to be free seeking the sun

into the storm intrepid

i still dream

of even ground

tall children who are dreamers

born of dreams free

wild like a forest

filled with forever love

of life overflowing with

abundance growing straight

not bent nor broken whole

uncaged not scarred never bound

promise whispering in
every breath eyes
open tomorrow promised
i still dream

i still dream
flying free
i dream the rising
after free-falling

line of old ladies

when i line up

with the old women healer ladies

the sages hags grammies

sorceresses witches great

granny medicine women

when i line

up with the old women

with stars falling from my hair

my robe shall be shot with

moonbeams my heart will become

water mothering holding knowing

when i line up with the old women

by the river washing souls

singing life like a hymn i will

lay down my sword & shield

until that time

stone

sharpens steel

the line feminine

dedicated to my mama Ernestine, her mama Nettie, to Nettie's mama, Mama Connie, to my daughters Ebony & Ayodele, & my granddaughter Maleyah

we are the ocean

etching the line that is

the shore

we are the line

we are the shore

we are the ocean

calling always rising tides

falling to rise again

we are the ocean

the line feminine

from whence they come

we bring them forth

tend mend & grow them

into women into men

we are the ocean

etching the line that is the shore

we are

the line

we are the shore

we are the line from which

they rise

the bosoms

on which they fall

we are the line of women

opening wider than ocean to bring forth

the family human to dwell upon the earth

we bring them forth

tend mend & grow them

into women into men

we are the shore

constantly calling for the ocean

remembering its embrace

before we had form or face

in its vastness we knew

we were the dreams of god

we understood

the distance from the ocean

the strength of the line

the world of need on the shore

we are from whence they come

we bring them forth

we tend & we mend

we grow them

into women into men

we are the line feminine

both ocean & shore

we are fruit on the vine

the oceans roar

the rainbows iridescence

salt in the sea

we are

as long as is

is

until is

is

is

no more

the line

the ocean

the shore

reading guide

*language as oppressor/the uppercase
& capitalism /not/puncturing the narrative
with traditional marks*

it is said that for a language to be valid it needs an army. english carries within its rules & regulations a worldview. according to george lakoff, the english language is built upon warlike metaphors.

have you ever considered the fact that all disciplines have a language particular to their practice. there is a language particular to medicine, law, science, & the arts. it stands to reason there is also a language of oppression.

throughout this book language is a contested ground in which the poet uses it as a weapon & a balm:

- see if you can find work where words are offered to soothe, heal & encourage
- can you find poems where the poet uses words to gather a force against the things that oppress the poet
- can you identify what the poet worldview is—what poems help to make the case

in this book of verse words are freed from punctuation & capitalization & are made to work in the service of counternarratives intended to undo what ink has done in the psyche of the reader. in ink we engage the dissonance between written & oral language. in the poem inked we engage the visual elements of language that feed stereotypes & offer the story behind the story the observer/reader thinks he knows.

these poems aim to break colonial rule/s in order to free the narratives of thriving. these are tales from a different center in which things are valued differently.

erotemes & virgules—containing the questions anew & identifying them early

when food is served on a different plate does it taste different. how can a writer make you look at their work differently. what happens when you are instructed to regard questions as questions before they are posed & others appear without conventional punctuation marks—does it order the importance of presented questions. do you feel you understand what the poet is saying or wants you to consider by rearranging the way you take in the poems. does it bother you & if so, why.

there are many poems that introduce the differently-place question mark within slashes—a bracketed & prime placement as to emphasize what is coming. here are some poems to discuss & look at to see visually how disruptive or helpful this new usage may be:

- "on mamas" (p. 177)
- "woman" (p. 183)
- "brother brother" (p. 187)
- "race" (p. 197)

cain & abel—origin of fratricide, of biblical proportions

in this collection are poems in which the poet considers the moral aspects of oppression & how it is possible to see the ethics of individuals and institutions in their action or lack of action. the poet calls attention to our duty to one another beyond race & class as humans & asks us to take responsibility for knowing what's done by institutions such as governments in our name. the poet challenges us to push back against things we understand as counter to human thriving & the poet is calling on us to decide where power lies & to suggest that we co-create the world we inhabit by our action or inaction. here are a few poems which do this calling on:

- "inked" (p. 66)
- "unsaid" (p. 75)
- "unwritten" (p. 79)
- "rendition" (p. 112)

perhaps there are others you have identified & within which you can explore these ideas.

heritage & breaking free of certain line/ages

everything is an evolution. even if at a point there is less than there was before it did not devolve to its present state.. instead it evolved to the state in which it is found. evolution should not be considered as linear.

becomings are not always comprehensible in a straight line. things come in waves & circles. therefore the thought of a continuum comes naturally. the poet is in conversation with previous poets, current events, lived reality, & she intentionally samples thought through intertextual connections with others across disciplines & time. the poet is distinctly unappreciative of genre & feels it is oppressive, prescriptive, & it function seeks to confer status on some art while denying it to others. she is from a line of poets who firmly believe in a black aesthetic & functions within the continuum of the black arts movement, which according to those who canonize art work, ended decades ago. this is the thing about what's written in ink—it doesn't have to tell the truth. everything in this book is written for the page & to be performed on stage. the work often changes on stage as the times change & like the tale of a griot it needs to fit a particular event—spit can do that.

explore the page & the performative in reading the following poems, both silently & aloud:

- "unwritten" (p. 79)
- "the artist" (p. 92)
- "dead poets" (p. 97)
- "the people (parts 1–3)" (pp. 151–157)

american dreamtime & shiny shit

the poet launches an assault on capitalism & consumerism & urges a valuing of the natural & the unreplicable by suggesting that the affection for material things is a distraction from things that should matter to humans. the poet considers american identity & the crisis of patriotism as it meets racial injustice. the poet challenges the concept of america to be in conversation with its unabridged story. the poet engages parts of american history in a conversation with issues that are currently in the news. shiny shit & money are looked at as tools of oppression utilized to dope the masses into sheep-like compliance with wolf movement.

the poems below are a few examples of this assault & consideration
& engagement:

- "voting : 2016" (p. 99)
- "polytricks" (p. 192)
- "race" (p. 197)
- "99 swang" (p. 213)

cultural warriors & gendered responsivity

tilting at patriarchy & entertaining the divine feminie the poet seeks to decolonize gender in these poems. the poet is concerned with the elevation of the human circle of yin & yang & conjuring profound wholeness in which humanity is interconnected & embedded within nature. the poet embraces the trope of family in a recasting that centers black lived experiences, language, & worldviews from the perspective of the ordinary to help look closely at extraordinary existential considerations.

look at the poems below as language that aims to address matriarchal & patriarchal systems as historical events & /un/fixed roles:

- "rendition" (p. 112)
- "the dime" (p. 135)
- "line of old ladies" (p. 241)
- "the line feminine" (p. 242)

acknowledgments

i give praise & thanks to my egun egun, my ori, & the orisa.

i am thankful for crossroads, for prayer with moving hands, & the knowledge that forward is the only true direction. i pay juba to the shoulders on which i stand. i am thankful for being.

i am thankful for being raised by lions & having them set my place at the table of the continuum, & ensuring that i was fed. i am grateful that when i have needed teachers, they have always appeared.

i am grateful for memory, grateful for being born with assignments, grateful the veil lifted & i remembered what was whispered in my ear before my first breath.

i offer my eternal gratitude to marvin x jackmon for baptizing me in fire; to amiri baraka who told me to pour forth without ceasing; to jean damu who told me not to idolize either of the former; to sonia sanchez for telling me, "god gave something to everyone & he gave you words"; to robert chrisman, who showed me the pendulum swinging always; ali ar rasheed for helping me to turn the ivory tower a beautiful blue black shade of ebony; to ngũgĩ wa thiong'o who confirmed for me the need to free myself from english; & to nathan hare for observing my manumission & dubbing my style as *ebonic euronics*. i offer a special thanks to august wilson who I began an affair with after his death. our walk together led me through the slave pens, across the graveyard, in the ocean home—to my truest self. deep bow to nedra t williams for spiritual guidance, connection, recognition, & other invaluable diviner

black magic woman gifts that continue to feed my soul, spirit, & mind.

i am grateful to nomadic press for enabling my conversation in the storm. special thanks to j. k. fowler for the ship on which we sail; his quiet thoughtfulness, & his love of beauty-filled quiet stillness & bright red fast moving thought. abundant gratitude to my brilliant & patient editor michalea mullin, who gracefully sank into my world & helped to afford me the space to see it more clearly.

thank you to my children upon whom i dream, for selecting such a volatile vessel. when i search for meaning i see your faces. i wish strength & fierceness to my beautiful daughters & to my suns' grace & peace. may you be invincible & always fall forward.

to my loved ones dead yet present, unborn yet promised, living now unseen & those steadfastly holding my dreams with me—we will make it home; no matter how long the road. the spark will never die. we will be whole, free, & altogether beautiful in perpetual harmony with the world. from my pen to all powers that listen—aluta continua. & to my co-conspirators standing with me in the storm; may these words be both bread & bullets.

finally, thank you to the following publications, where the following poems were published in earlier forms: "women," in *black magnolias journal*; "canon" & "inked," in *performing literacy: a narrative inquiry into performance pedagogy in a marginalized community*.

ayodele nzinga

holds an MFA in Writing and Consciousness and a PhD in Transformative Learning. Her chapbook *The Horse Eaters* was published by Nomadic Press, her work can be found in *Vision Magazine*, two volumes of the *Journal of Pan African Studies, 14 Hills Journal, Magnolia Journal*, in the anthologies *Environmental Terrorist* and *The Say it Loud*. Nzinga is a Helen Crocker Russell awardee, a member of Alameda County Women's Hall of Fame. In another life she is the founder of Oakland's oldest Black theater company, Lower Bottom Playaz—recognized by the August Wilson House as the only director to direct the August Wilson Century Cycle in chronological order, and the producer of BAMBDFEST. She is Oakland's first Poet Laureate. ayodelenzinga.com

OTHER WAYS TO SUPPORT NOMADIC PRESS' WRITERS

In 2020, two funds geared specifically toward supporting our writers were created: the **Nomadic Press Black Writers Fund** and the **Nomadic Press Emergency Fund**.

The former is a forever fund that puts money directly into the pockets of our Black writers. The latter provides dignity-centered emergency grants to any of our writers in need.

Please consider supporting these funds. You can also more generally support Nomadic Press by donating to our general fund via nomadicpress.org/donate and by continuing to buy our books. As always, thank you for your support!

Scan below for more information and/or to donate.
You can also donate at nomadicpress.org/store.